2024-Super Delicious
Anti-Inflammatory Diet
Cookbook for Beginners

Healthy Meal Plans and Dishes for a Healthy You

Jennifer Phillip

Copyright © 2024 by Jennifer Phillip

All rights reserved. Except for brief quotations included in critical reviews and certain other noncommercial uses allowed by copyright law, no part of this publication may be reproduced, distributed, or transmitted in any form or by any means, including photocopying, recording, or other electronic or mechanical methods, without the publisher's prior written permission.

Table of contents

Contents

CHAPTER ONE 7
    Overview of Anti-Inflammatory Diets 7
    The Benefits and Dangers Of Inflammation 7
    The Benefits Of Inflammation 7
    The Dangers Of Inflammation 8
    Principles Of The Anti- Inflammatory Diet 11
    Smart Dietary Choices 12
    Anti-Inflammatory Foods 13
    Guidelines for An Anti-Inflammatory Diet 18
    Foods That Worsen Inflammation 20
    Unique Bodies, Unique Reactions To Food 21
    Foods To Enjoy 24
    Foods To Consider With Care 26
CHAPTER TWO 28
    Preparing For A Healthy Change 28
    An Optimistic Outlook 28
    All Set To Go! 30
    Conclusion: 31
    The Anti-Inflammatory Pantry And Kitchen 32
    Your Essential Anti-Inflammatory Supply 32
    Canned, Jarred, And Bagged Foods 33
    Cooking With Efficiency 33
    Arsenal Of Time-Saving Tools 35
TIPS FOR STORING FOOD: 36
TIPS REHEATING FOOD: 37
    Chronic Inflammation-Free Living 38
    Understanding Chronic Inflammation: 38
    Lifestyle Strategies For Chronic Inflammation-Free Living: 39
    Additional Considerations: 39
Weekly Meal Plans with Recipes 42

CHAPTER THREE 43
Week 1 Meal Plan And Recipes 43
WEEK 1 MEAL PLAN 44
WEEK 1 SHOPPING 45
OPTIONAL WEEKLY PREP GUIDE 47
breakfast 49
- Avocado Toast with Poached Eggs – BREAKFAST 50
- Berry and Chia Smoothie – BREAKFAST 52
- Oatmeal with Almonds and Blueberries – BREAKFAST 53
- Greek Yogurt with Honey and Walnuts – BREAKFAST 54
- Green Tea and Banana Pancakes – BREAKFAST 55
- Scrambled Tofu with Spinach and Tomatoes – BREAKFAST 57
- Smoothie Bowl with Mixed Berries and Seeds – BREAKFAST 59

LUNCH 60
- Quinoa Salad with Mixed Vegetables – LUNCH 61
- Turmeric Chicken Soup – LUNCH 63
- Lentil Salad with Arugula and Feta – LUNCH 64
- Chickpea and Avocado Wrap – LUNCH 65
- Kale Caesar Salad with Grilled Chicken – LUNCH 66
- Soba Noodle Bowl with Edamame and Ginger Broth – LUNCH 68
- Roasted Vegetable and Hummus Sandwich – LUNCH 69

DINNER 70
- Grilled Salmon with Steamed Broccoli – DINNER 71
- Zucchini Noodles with Pesto and Cherry Tomatoes – DINNER 73
- Baked Cod with Asparagus and Sweet Potato – DINNER 74
- Stuffed Bell Peppers with Quinoa and Black Beans – DINNER 75
- Eggplant Parmesan with a Side of Mixed Greens – DINNER 76
- Moroccan Chicken Stew with Couscous – DINNER 77
- Grilled Trout with Quinoa and Roasted Carrots – DINNER 79

Chapter Four 81
Week 2 Meal Plan and Recipes 81
WEEK 2 MEAL PLAN 82
Week to Shopping List 83

WEEKLY 2 OPTIONAL PREP GUIDE 84

WEEK 2 RECIPES 86

BREAKFAST 87

    Spinach and Mushroom Omelet – BREAKFAST 88

    Almond Butter and Banana Smoothie – BREAKFAST 89

    Greek Yogurt with Mixed Nuts and Honey – BREAKFAST 90

    Apple Cinnamon Oatmeal – BREAKFAST 91

    Blueberry and Almond Pancakes – BREAKFAST 92

    Avocado and Egg Breakfast Pizza – BREAKFAST 93

    Chia Pudding with Fresh Berries – BREAKFAST 94

LUNCH 95

    Avocado Chicken Salad – LUNCH 96

    Lentil Soup with Kale – LUNCH 97

    Quinoa Stuffed Peppers – LUNCH 98

    Turkey and Spinach Wrap – LUNCH 99

    Mediterranean Chickpea Salad – LUNCH 100

    Roasted Beet and Goat Cheese Salad – LUNCH 101

    Vegetable and Hummus Tartine – LUNCH 102

DINNER 103

    Turmeric Roasted Chicken with Cauliflower – DINNER 104

    Grilled Shrimp with Garlic Broccoli – DINNER 105

    Baked Trout with Lemon and Dill – DINNER 107

    Beef Stir-Fry with Bell Peppers and Broccoli – DINNER 108

    Herb-Crusted Salmon with Asparagus – DINNER 109

    Lamb Chops with Mint Pesto and Roasted Veggies – DINNER 110

    Pesto Pasta with Sun-Dried Tomatoes and Pine Nuts – DINNER 111

WEEK 3 MEAL PLAN 112

WEEK 3 SHOPPING LIST 113

OPTIONAL WEEKLY PREP GUIDE 115

WEEK 3 RECIPES 117

BREAKFAST 119

    Chia Coconut Yogurt Parfait – BREAKFAST 120

    Avocado Berry Smoothie – BREAKFAST 121

- Pumpkin Oatmeal – BREAKFAST 122
- Toasted Almond Butter and Banana Sandwich – BREAKFAST 123
- Green Detox Smoothie – BREAKFAST 124
- Egg White Omelet with Spinach and Mushrooms – BREAKFAST 125
- Oatmeal with Apples and Cinnamon – BREAKFAST 126

LUNCH 127
- Broccoli and Almond Soup – LUNCH 128
- Roast Beef Wrap with Arugula and Horseradish – LUNCH 130
- Lentil and Vegetable Stew – LUNCH 131
- Sardine Salad on Whole Grain Toast – LUNCH 132
- Tomato and White Bean Salad – LUNCH 133
- Sweet Potato and Black Bean Chili – LUNCH 134
- Grilled Chicken Caesar Salad – LUNCH 135

DINNER 136
- Grilled Tuna Steaks with Olive Tapenade – DINNER 137
- Stuffed Acorn Squash with Quinoa and Cranberries – DINNER 138
- Rosemary Lemon Chicken with Roasted Brussels Sprouts – DINNER 139
- Thai Coconut Curry with Tofu and Vegetables – DINNER 141
- Baked Salmon with Dill and Lemon Asparagus – DINNER 142
- Herb Roasted Lamb with Root Vegetables – DINNER 143
- Pasta Primavera with Olive Oil and Vegetables – DINNER 144

APPENDIX A 145
CONVERSION TABLES 145

CHAPTER ONE

OVERVIEW OF ANTI-INFLAMMATORY DIETS

Inflammation, which can take away our sense of well-being and cause a general slowdown, may be an indication that we have something wrong with our diet or lifestyle over a period of time. Normal inflammation within the body is a sign of health as it helps in maintaining the right balance of the internal environment. The only time when this process becomes problematic is when it exceeds normal limits. This chapter will explain how this happens.

We will also give you the basics of an elementary anti-inflammatory diet plan that is based on whole foods and backed up by scientific research to help you get your natural balance back. Additionally, by using our simple lists of what to eat and what not to, you can choose meals much beyond the recipes presented here. We will also look at how different compounds affect people's bodies and how to modify these recipes for your specific dietary needs.

The Benefits and Dangers Of Inflammation

In the immense human immune system that exists, inflammation is a fundamental process. Essentially, inflammation is protection for the body; it tries and guards itself by getting rid of things that can cause harm such as damaged cells or irritants and beginning to heal. Although this delicate balance between safeguarding and endangering has always been known to be true, these days we also realize more than ever before just how many diseases can come from chronic inflammations. This piece of writing will go through all the complexities involved with inflaming topics- both good points/bad points; including what they are etc., but mainly focuses on their importance towards general wellbeing.

The Benefits Of Inflammation

Immediate Protective Response

The main function of inflammation is for protection and good. It is the immediate reaction of the body to infection or injury. The redness, heat, swelling, pain and often loss of function that characterize acute inflammation reflect the immune system coming into play. These signs are not just random; every one of them has a role in the healing process. For example, more blood flowing through an area (redness and heat) brings necessary nutrients and immune cells there; swelling caused by fluid build-up helps isolate it – thus containing any potential pathogens from spreading elsewhere within the body.

Initiating Healing

Once you have controlled an infection or cleaned up debris from a wound, the body is signaled by inflammation to start repairing the damaged tissues. This means that cells are replaced, new tissue is made and sometimes scar forms. If there were no inflammations, wounds will not heal properly and infections may end up being fatal.

Protection Against Pathogens

In order to survive, the body has a variety of defenders against different forms of life. These attackers may include dead cells or various types of bacteria among other things. To identify and destroy these hazardous organisms, antibodies are released by some of the immune system's other cells. Still others create chemical substances which can attack them directly or proteins that will fight off these intruders. This reactive process is important because without it one would not live for very long due to all the harmful pathogens in our environment getting past our defenses through inflammation which activates many immune cells and substances aimed at nullifying dangerous pathogens.

The Dangers Of Inflammation

To exist, the body has an array of guards against different kinds of beings. These invaders might be dead cells or many forms of germs and so on. Some other cells of the immune system release antibodies to recognize and destroy these perilous living things. Once they are identified as hazardous organisms, some others manufacture chemicals that can directly attack them or proteins that will resist such intruders. This is crucial because in its absence one would die very soon since all harmful pathogens around us get through our defences by means of inflammation that activates lots of immune cells and substances designed to counteract dangerous pathogens.

Chronic Diseases

Chronic inflammation has been linked to numerous diseases, including heart disease, diabetes, cancer, arthritis, and neurodegenerative conditions like Alzheimer's disease. In these cases, the inflammatory response, instead of resolving, continues unabated, often due to an ongoing injury, irritation, or an autoimmune disorder where the body mistakenly attacks its tissues. For instance, in the case of atherosclerosis, a condition that can lead to heart attacks and strokes, chronic inflammation plays a central role. The buildup of fatty deposits in the walls of arteries triggers an inflammatory response. Over time, this can lead to the narrowing and hardening of arteries, compromising blood flow.

Autoimmune Disorders

When the immune system can't recognize its own cells and destroys them as if they were foreign substances, an autoimmune disease occurs. Rheumatoid arthritis, lupus erythematosus and multiple sclerosis have in common that they cause long-lasting inflammation as a result of autoimmunity. Persistent vigilance injures organs while at the same time weakening defensive powers thereby exposing us to opportunistic infections.

Contributing to Mental Health Issues

New studies show that long-term inflammation may be tied to mental health problems such as depression and anxiety. Inflammation can change alertness, mood, and cognition by affecting the brain's chemistry and working though how exactly is not well understood yet. But one thing is certain; immune system functions have a lot to do with brain health.

Balancing the Scale

As much as it is dual in nature, the problem of controlling inflammation therefore lies in finding a balance. Among other things, lifestyle and diet are significant determinants of body response to inflammation. The risk for chronic inflammation can be minimized by engaging in regular exercise, eating food stuffs that are rich in antioxidants which include fruits vegetables and omega three fatty acids, as well as getting enough sleep.

It has also been proven that medical interventions have an important role to play when dealing with chronic inflammations. In most cases anti inflammatory drugs like Non steroidal Anti Inflammatory Drugs (NSAIDs), corticosteroids or even natural supplements such as turmeric and fish oil are prescribed to manage swellings. Nevertheless these methods have their own shortcomings hence showing why treatment should cover all aspects of one's life instead only considering modifications on how they live it due to heightened levels caused by stress that may be countered through practices like mindfulness towards oneself or yoga exercises followed by meditation which eventually lead into having positive effects on reducing levels of inflammations among individuals

Conclusion

Inflammation is where health meets illness, representing the contradiction of being a necessary reaction as well as a possible danger. It is important to know how complicated inflammation can be, recognizing its usefulness during short-term situations and dealing with it if it becomes long-lasting in order to stay healthy overall. Taking up this tightrope walk between protective and destructive roles played by inflammation requires us to live in ways that foster a balanced immune response while using interventions cautiously within medical settings; thereby striving towards balance within complex organic systems of our bodies.

Recent studies have connected many illnesses and health issues, such as the following to chronic inflammation by certain cancers.

- Rheumatoid Arthritis (RA)
- Ankylosing Spondylitis (AS).
- Type 2 Diabetes.
- Heart disease
- High blood pressure (hypertension).
- Crohn's disease
- Inflammatory bowel disease.
- Asthma
- Chronic Obstructive Pulmonary Disease (COPD).
- Depression and Anxiety.
- Alzheimer's disease and Parkinson's disease.

Principles Of The Anti- Inflammatory Diet

The anti-inflammatory diet is a blueprint for nutrition created to decrease inflammation and enhance general health. The core of it focuses on eating a range of whole nutrient-dense foods and limiting processed diets, sugars and saturated fats which can worsen inflammation. Vital points are fruits and vegetables – high in antioxidants and phytonutrients that fight oxidative stress; a major cause of inflammatory conditions.

Another component is whole grains, legumes as well as nuts that provide necessary fiber to support digestive system functioning while reducing levels of inflammatory markers.

Omega-3 fatty acids found in fatty fish such as salmon or mackerel, flaxseeds and walnuts play a central role because they have anti-inflammatory effects unlike omega sixes which should be taken with care because too much may result into more inflammation than necessary. Poultry, tofu, beans etc., contain low amounts of fats but higher amounts protein compared to red meats like beef lamb which are associated with increased levels of C-reactive protein (CRP) – an indicator for systemic inflammation in the body. Moreover, various herbs spices especially turmeric ginger among others are known to possess strong anti-inflammatories properties thus making them important parts of this diet too. Hydration cannot be ignored either since water herbal teas as well as other non-sugary beverages keep the body adequately hydrated while supporting detoxification processes at cellular levels throughout all organ systems involved; therefore even though its primary aim is reduction or prevention against inflammations but also seeks overall improvement in health status by ensuring balance between intake output energy nutrients required for optimal physiological functioning within human beings themselves.

Smart Dietary Choices

Making smart dietary choices is pivotal in maintaining optimal health, preventing chronic diseases, and ensuring that our body functions at its best. At the core, it's about choosing foods that nourish the body, provide essential nutrients, and support bodily functions. Here are key principles to guide smart dietary choices:

1. **Prioritize Whole Foods:** Focus on foods that are minimally processed. Whole fruits, vegetables, grains, nuts, and seeds are packed with vitamins, minerals, fiber, and antioxidants that are essential for health.

2. **Balance Your Plate:** Aim for a balanced diet that includes a variety of food groups. Incorporate lean proteins, healthy fats, and complex carbohydrates into each meal to ensure a range of nutrients.

3. **Limit Added Sugars and Processed Foods:** Foods high in added sugars and heavily processed foods often contain empty calories and lack nutritional value. They can contribute to weight gain, inflammation, and chronic diseases.

4. **Stay Hydrated:** Water is essential for nearly every bodily function, including digestion and elimination of toxins. Drinking adequate amounts of water daily is crucial for maintaining health.

5. **Mindful Eating:** Pay attention to your eating habits. Eating slowly and being mindful of the taste, texture, and smell of your food can improve digestion and satisfaction with meals.

6. **Incorporate Healthy Fats:** Not all fats are created equal. Monounsaturated and polyunsaturated fats, found in avocados, nuts, seeds, and fish, can improve heart health and enhance nutrient absorption.

7. **Opt for Lean Proteins:** Choosing lean protein sources, such as poultry, fish, legumes, and tofu, can provide essential nutrients without the excess saturated fats found in some meats.

8. **Increase Fiber Intake:** Foods high in fiber, such as whole grains, fruits, vegetables, and legumes, can improve digestive health, help control blood sugar levels, and aid in weight management.

9. **Limit Sodium and Salt Intake:** High sodium consumption can lead to hypertension and cardiovascular diseases. Opting for fresh foods over processed foods can significantly reduce sodium intake.

10. **Plan and Prepare:** Planning meals and snacks in advance can help you make healthier choices and avoid the temptation of fast food or processed snacks.

By embracing these principles, individuals can make smart dietary choices that support their health and well-being. It's about creating a sustainable, enjoyable approach to eating that nourishes the body and satisfies the palate.

Anti-Inflammatory Foods

1. Barries
2. Fatty Fish
3. Leafy Greens
4. Nuts
5. Olive Oil
6. Turmeric
7. Ginger
8. Green Tea
9. Tomatoes
10. Peppers
11. Whole Grain
12. Dark Chocolate
13. Beets
14. Avocado
15. Garlic

Berries

Types of berries such as strawberries, blueberries, raspberries and blackberries are full with vitamins, minerals, fibers and antioxidants that makes them a nutritional powerhouse. Additionally anthocyanins specifically are responsible for the colours seen in these fruits and also contribute to their anti-inflammatory properties. These elements help to fight against inflammations thereby reducing chances of getting sick while at the same time improving one's immunity. Consumption of berries on regular basis has been linked to lowering heart disease risk factors like blood pressure; they can also help with mental health improvement. Including various kinds into your meals may be as easy as throwing some on top of morning oatmeal or making smoothie out them or even having them around for snack time because they are healthy snacks too..

Fatty Fish

Omega-3 fatty acids, which are composed of EPA and DHA fats known for their anti-inflammatory effects, are found in fatty fish like salmon, mackerel, sardines, and trout. These kinds of fats can lower the quantities of inflammatory markers inside the body such as CRP (C-reactive protein), thereby safeguarding us against heart disease as well as brain aging or other inflammation-related illnesses. In addition to keeping our hearts healthy omega threes may also help with mental health; therefore it is suggested that people should eat oily fish at least twice per week because this can also reduce chronic illness risks too. Fatty fish can be taken a number of times throughout one's life so they remain healthy inside themselves all throughout their lives even into old age but if someone doesn't want to do this then taking omega 3 supplements may be an option although it is always better getting your nutrients from whole foods where possible especially those who don't eat meat.

Leafy Greens

Spinach, kale, and collard greens are all very healthy because they have vitamins A, C, E and K as well as antioxidants and fiber which makes them effective anti-inflammatory foods. These nutrients fight inflammation together and also guard against oxidative stress that can cause chronic disease. Moreover, leafy vegetables contain a lot of vitamin K which is good for bones especially. You can eat more salads with these or put them in your smoothie or even add some to soup or casserole dishes if you want to get creative with how much you eat this type of food! Another reason why people should eat leafy greens regularly is because it lowers their chances of getting heart diseases; improves eyesight and digestion too!

Nuts

Almonds, walnuts, and others; in other words nuts are a good source of fats that are healthy, proteins, vitamins and minerals too. They contain antioxidants and omega-3 fatty acids which help fight inflammation. Fiber is also found in abundance within nuts therefore aiding weight loss as well as supporting digestive system health leading to less inflammations. Cardiovascular diseases like diabetes or cancer have been shown to be less likely when people eat nuts regularly. This means that besides being just tasty snacks you can sprinkle over salads or put into dishes while cooking; they still offer many benefits for our bodies which contribute towards having an overall anti-inflammatory diet.

Olive Oil

The Mediterranean diet relies heavily on virgin olive oil which is also referred as Extra. This is because it has anti-inflammatory properties and promotes a healthier heart. The reason behind this is that it contains oleocanthal, an antioxidant compound with ibuprofen-like effects against inflammation. It can thus be used to treat or prevent many chronic diseases such as cancer among others; additionally it helps lower blood pressure levels as well as reducing risks of some cancers too . You can easily incorporate olive oil into your meals by using it in cooking like sautéing vegetables, making salad dressings or even substituting butter with this healthy fat source but don't forget about the antioxidants so always go for extra virgin types!

Turmeric

Curcuma, an Asian spice that is yellow in color contains curcumin which is a strong antioxidant and anti-inflammatory element. Some anti-inflammatory medications are matched by curcumin but without the side effects. It aids in bringing down swellings connected to arthritis, diabetes etc. Unfortunately, it is not easily absorbed into the bloodstream hence necessary to take it with piperine from black pepper which improves its absorption rate. There are various ways of introducing turmeric into your meals such as using it for cooking curry or soup among others even blending with smoothies can work too.

Ginger

For ages, ginger has been known as a strong spice that fights inflammation. Gingerol, one of its components, is highly anti-inflammatory and antioxidant. Ginger has been shown to reduce muscle pain and soreness, symptoms of osteoarthritis, menstrual cramps among other pains. It may also decrease blood sugar levels as well as risk markers for cardiovascular diseases such as cholesterol levels. This versatile ingredient can be eaten fresh or used in powder form while cooking; it can also be taken orally through capsules like supplements or even added into drinks like tea blends and smoothies for extra anti-inflammatory power.

Green Tea

Green tea is one of the healthiest drinks. It has lots of antioxidants and phytochemicals that bring down inflammation. The most important active ingredient in green tea is epigallocatechin gallate (EGCG). It was found to cut inflammation and shield cells from harm. Drinking green tea regularly is associated with lowered chances of heart disease, cancer, Alzheimer's, obesity and other inflammatory diseases too. To get maximum antioxidant power from it, take two to three cups a day without much processing.

Tomatoes

Lycopene is an antioxidant that makes tomatoes red and has anti-inflammatory properties. Cooking tomatoes release more useful lycopene therefore tomato sauces, soups or pastes are good sources of this nutrient. Tomatoes also have potassium, vitamin C, vitamin K and folate which add up to their health benefits including lower chances for cancer and heart diseases too. You can increase your consumption of anti-inflammatory compounds by eating different types of fresh as well as cooked tomatoes.

Peppers

Vitamins A and C are antioxidants that relieve inflammation; therefore, bell peppers and chili peppers can be taken as a great source of them. Capsaicin is contained in chili pepper, which is a chemical that could relieve pain as well as inflammation. Unlike this component of quercetin represents an antioxidant in bell pepper that may lower markers for chronic didisease-related inflammations among individuals with such conditions. It's worth noting that not only does adding different types of these vegetables into your meal plan make it more colorful but also healthier too because they have many health benefits such as: preventing cancer cells from growing too fast or reducing cholesterol levels in the body.

Whole Grains

Entire grains, opposed to processed ones, have all portions of the grain remaining in it thus becoming a good source for vitamins, minerals and fiber. C-reactive protein which is an inflammation marker in the blood can be lowered by fibers obtained from whole grains. Intake of whole grains on a regular basis is linked with decreased chances of suffering from heart diseases, type 2 diabetes, obesity among other types cancers also. Making the switch from refined to whole-wheat products is an easy way to improve your health.

Dark Chocolate

Dark chocolate is rich in antioxidants, such as flavonoids that possess anti-inflammatory effects. Eating dark chocolate moderately may enhance cardiac well-being, improve insulin resistance and lower down inflammation levels. Nevertheless, one must select dark chocolates containing not less than 70% cocoa and eat them sparingly so as not to consume too much sugar or calories at once.

Beets

Beets aren't just red and tasty: they are packed with nutrients, including fibre, vitamin C and potassium. Often referred to as betalain-containing vegetables – these pigments have anti-inflammatory traits hence helpful in reducing inflammation in the body and protecting it against heart diseases or cancerous cells. Roasted, boiled or grated into salads are some of the ways you can eat them!

Avocado

Avocado is rich in fiber, magnesium, and potassium as well as monounsaturated fats that all contribute to their anti-inflammatory properties. They also have substances that could lower inflammation among new cells forming the skin. Avocado can help with cholesterol levels, lower the chance of heart disease and increase the uptake of antioxidants. They are flexible enough to be included into salads or sandwiches; blended into smoothies or used instead of butter when baking.

Garlic

For centuries, garlic has been used for its healing powers particularly when it comes to fighting inflammation. It contains a medicaments substance called diallyl disulfide which can reduce the chemicals produced by the body that indicate swelling is occurring. In addition to this ability, garlic also helps strengthen immunity, lower high blood pressure levels, and safeguard against cardiovascular diseases. Moreover, you can easily include garlic into your meals as it goes well with various recipes and adds taste.

Including these foods that fight inflammation in your meals can help reduce inflammation and improve health in general. To gain from all their different nutrients and antioxidants, it is necessary to consume a wide array of them.

Guidelines for An Anti-Inflammatory Diet

Adopting an anti-inflammatory diet involves focusing on foods known to reduce inflammation while minimizing intake of those that can aggravate it. Here are key guidelines to follow for an anti-inflammatory diet:

1. Emphasize Fruits and Vegetables

Prioritize a colorful array of fruits and vegetables. These foods are high in natural antioxidants and polyphenols—protective compounds that reduce inflammation. Aim for at least 5-9 servings per day, incorporating a variety of colors to ensure a wide range of nutrients.

2. Incorporate Healthy Fats

Choose sources of healthy fats that have anti-inflammatory properties, such as olive oil, avocados, and fatty fish rich in omega-3 fatty acids (e.g., salmon, mackerel, and sardines). Nuts and seeds, like walnuts, flaxseeds, and chia seeds, are also excellent choices.

3. Select Whole Grains Over Refined

Opt for whole grains like oats, quinoa, brown rice, and barley instead of refined grains. Whole grains have more fiber, which can help reduce levels of C-reactive protein (a marker of inflammation) in the blood.

4. Limit Processed Foods and Sugars

Processed foods and added sugars can spike blood sugar levels and lead to increased inflammation. Minimize intake of sugary beverages, sweets, and processed snacks.

5. Incorporate Spices and Herbs

Many herbs and spices, including turmeric (with its active component curcumin) and ginger, have potent anti-inflammatory effects. Use these generously to flavor your food.

6. Choose Lean Protein Sources

Opt for lean protein sources, such as chicken, turkey, beans, and lentils. If you consume red meat, select lean cuts and limit your intake.

7. Hydrate Properly

Drink plenty of water throughout the day. Staying hydrated helps your body remove toxins and reduce inflammation. Herbal teas can also be a good option.

8. Limit Alcohol and Caffeine

Excessive consumption of alcohol and caffeine can contribute to inflammation. Moderation is key, with a preference for red wine, known for its antioxidant properties, if alcohol is to be consumed.

9. Focus on Gut Health

Incorporate fermented foods rich in probiotics, like yogurt, kefir, sauerkraut, and kombucha, to support gut health. A healthy gut flora can help reduce inflammation throughout the body.

10. Plan Balanced Meals

Ensure that each meal is balanced, incorporating components from different food groups. For example, a plate could include a lean protein source, a portion of whole grains, and a variety of vegetables dressed with healthy fats.

11. Practice Mindful Eating

Pay attention to your body's hunger and satiety signals. Eating mindfully can prevent overeating and reduce stress-related eating, which can contribute to inflammation.

12. Monitor Your Body's Response

Everyone's body reacts differently to foods. Pay attention to how your body responds to certain foods and adjust your diet accordingly. Some individuals may find they are sensitive to gluten or dairy, which can cause inflammation.

By adhering to these guidelines, the anti-inflammatory diet can help manage inflammation, reduce the risk of chronic diseases, promote overall health, and improve quality of life. Remember, making gradual changes and choosing foods you enjoy are key to sustainable, long-term dietary habits.

Foods That Worsen Inflammation

Some foods and eating behaviors might cause chronic inflammation that can make worse conditions of disease linked to it including heart diseases, diabetes, arthritis amongst many others. Enumerated below are types of meals that can heighten levels of inflammation in the body:

1. Sugar and High-fructose Corn Syrup

Foods and beverages high in sugar and high-fructose corn syrup, such as soft drinks, candies, and baked goods, can significantly increase inflammation. Excessive consumption of these sugars triggers the release of inflammatory messengers known as cytokines.

2. Artificial Trans Fats

Trans fats are among the most inflammatory fats. They're found in partially hydrogenated oils, a type of manufactured fat used in some margarines, snack foods, and packaged baked goods to extend shelf life. Unlike natural trans fats found in dairy and meats, artificial trans fats are strongly linked to inflammation and heart disease.

3. Refined Carbohydrates

White bread, white pasta, and many processed foods made with refined flour have a high glycemic index. They can spike blood sugar levels, leading to an inflammatory response. Refined carbohydrates have had most of their fiber removed, reducing their nutritional value and increasing inflammatory effects.

4. Excessive Alcohol

Moderate alcohol consumption might have some health benefits, but excessive drinking can cause severe inflammation. It can lead to a condition known as "leaky gut," where toxins enter the bloodstream through the intestinal lining, leading to widespread inflammation.

5. Processed Meat

Processed meats, such as sausages, bacon, ham, and smoked meats, contain more advanced glycation end products (AGEs) than most other meats. AGEs are formed through certain cooking methods and are known to induce inflammation.

6. Vegetable and Seed Oils

Some vegetable oils, like soybean, corn, and sunflower oils, are high in omega-6 fatty acids. While omega-6s are essential in moderation, an imbalance of omega-6s to omega-3s in the diet can lead to inflammation.

7. Fried Foods

Fried foods contain high levels of AGEs due to their cooking process. Regular consumption of fried foods not only contributes to inflammation but also increases the risk of developing chronic diseases.

8. Artificial Additives

Some artificial additives, including aspartame and monosodium glutamate (MSG), can trigger inflammatory responses, especially in individuals sensitive to these substances. Foods containing these additives can include diet sodas, processed snacks, and fast food.

9. Dairy Products

For some individuals, dairy products can trigger an inflammatory response, particularly in those with a sensitivity or intolerance to lactose or casein, which are found in milk and dairy products.

10. Gluten-Containing Grains

People with gluten sensitivity or celiac disease experience inflammation when consuming gluten, a protein found in wheat, barley, and rye. Even in non-celiac individuals, gluten can sometimes contribute to inflammation.

To minimize inflammation, it's advisable to reduce the intake of these foods and consider alternatives that are less likely to promote inflammation. Shifting towards an anti-inflammatory diet rich in whole, nutrient-dense foods can significantly impact overall health and well-being.

Unique Bodies, Unique Reactions To Food

Nightshade plants: In case of arthritis or another inflammatory condition, it may be helpful to avoid tomatoes, potatoes, eggplants, and peppers.

Seeds & Nuts: Be careful if you have allergies and find substitutes when necessary.

Shellfish: This is a must-miss for those who are allergic because severe reactions can occur.

Gluten Grains: If gluten sensitive then switch to alternatives without it.

Dairy Product: For people with lactose intolerance or milk allergy should select lactose-free products or avoid them altogether.

Soy Products: Use sparingly in the presence of hormone-sensitive conditions such as breast cancer due to the estrogen-like effect produced by soybeans which contain natural compounds called isoflavones; these compounds bind with receptors on cells within certain tissues causing them to mimic actions normally elicited by actual hormones like estrogen thereby promoting growths of some cancers including those found in breast tissue.

Contrary to popular belief, food sensitivities and intolerances are not allergies at all because they do not engage the immune system. However, this research is growing but nebulous; for most people, food tolerance means how you feel after you've eaten it. Customize this diet to your needs no one knows your body better than you do. Keep a record of what happens when you eat a certain food and consult with a registered dietitian if you're unsure about whether or not it fits within your dietary restrictions.

Fish such as salmon and herring are rich in anti-inflammatory nutrients; these omega-3 fats fight inflammation throughout the body—and they're highly absorbable too. If seafood isn't off-limits for you (because of an allergy or other reason), make these two fish regulars on your menu plan each week.

Nuts like walnuts and cashews are bursting with anti-inflammatory compounds—not to mention their satisfying crunchy texture. Almonds have a little bit of protein along with healthy fats and vitamin E packed into each bite-sized piece; pecans offer similar benefits though in smaller amounts overall due to their lower calorie content per serving size compared with almond counterparts.

Most people can eat ancient grains without any problems — celiac disease or gluten intolerance aside, of course (in which case steer clear).

However strict elimination diets may exclude these types of carbs altogether since they're not necessary for most inflammation-reduction efforts anyway; that's why we list them under "Consider with Care" here instead where appropriate based on current knowledge about whole grain processing methods used by manufacturers such as flour milling techniques employed during production stages versus others like intact whole grain quinoa which reigns supreme among its peers thanks partly due its natural anti-inflammatory properties as well being complete protein source containing all essential amino acids humans need daily intake levels met easily through consumption alone when combined with other foods having similar nutritional profiles thus making them perfect candidates inclusion within an balanced healthy eating plan designed around reducing chronic low grade systemic inflammation levels seen so often today among modern populations worldwide.

In fact soy is not only a big allergen but also one heck of an anti-inflammatory fighter, contrary to popular belief. Soybeans actually have been shown in numerous studies as being able reduce risks for many types cancer including breast prostate colorectal etc these findings are absolutely amazing if you're someone like me who loves snacking on some steamed edamame at your favorite sushi bar!

Additionally this versatile food provides high amounts protein per serving size making it great choice vegetarians vegans alike looking meet their dietary needs without resorting animal products; moreover fibers found within soybeans can help regulate bowel movements thus preventing constipation further adding overall gut health benefits associated with consuming more fiber rich foods such beans peas lentils etc Eggs are packed vitamins like choline lutein however they're quite allergenic too though not necessarily anti-inflammatory themselves still good source quality complete proteins within balanced diet so don't cross them off just yet!

Dairy is another common offender when it comes down people having allergies towards certain types because there may be lactose intolerances involved which would then lead us to consider using low fat versions instead where possible since these tend contain less amounts saturated fats than full cream milk varieties do for example but let's take things step by shall we?

Foods To Enjoy

Adopting an anti-inflammatory diet involves focusing on foods that naturally combat inflammation in the body. This dietary approach can help reduce the risk of chronic diseases such as heart disease, arthritis, and diabetes. Here's a list of anti-inflammatory foods to enjoy:

Fruits

- **Berries**: Strawberries, blueberries, raspberries, and blackberries are rich in antioxidants and vitamins.
- **Cherries**: Especially tart cherries, are high in anthocyanins and antioxidants.
- **Oranges**: Packed with vitamin C and potassium, they help reduce inflammation and boost the immune system.
- **Pineapple**: Contains bromelain, an enzyme that may reduce inflammation and aid digestion.

Vegetables

- **Leafy Greens**: Spinach, kale, and collard greens offer high levels of vitamins and minerals.
- **Broccoli**: High in sulforaphane, an antioxidant with potent anti-inflammatory effects.
- **Beets**: Rich in antioxidants and can reduce inflammation.
- **Tomatoes**: Loaded with lycopene, especially when cooked, helping to reduce inflammation.

Healthy Fats

- **Avocados**: Full of monounsaturated fats, potassium, and magnesium.
- **Olives and Olive Oil**: Packed with heart-healthy monounsaturated fats and oleocanthal, which has properties similar to non-steroidal anti-inflammatory drugs.
- **Nuts**: Almonds and walnuts are high in omega-3 fatty acids, vitamin E, and magnesium.

Protein Sources

- **Fatty Fish**: Salmon, mackerel, sardines, and trout are excellent sources of omega-3 fatty acids.
- **Chia Seeds and Flaxseeds**: Vegetarian sources of omega-3s and fiber.

Whole Grains

- **Oats**: Rich in fiber, which can help reduce C-reactive protein levels in the blood.
- **Quinoa and Brown Rice**: Provide essential nutrients without promoting inflammation.

Spices and Herbs

- **Turmeric**: Contains curcumin, known for its anti-inflammatory and antioxidant properties. Best absorbed with black pepper.

- **Ginger**: Offers anti-inflammatory benefits and can reduce muscle pain and soreness.

- **Garlic**: Has been shown to have an anti-inflammatory effect on the body.

Beverages

- **Green Tea**: Packed with antioxidants, particularly epigallocatechin gallate (EGCG), which is known for its anti-inflammatory effects.

- **Bone Broth**: Rich in minerals and collagen, which can help reduce gut inflammation and heal the lining.

Incorporating these foods into your diet can help manage and reduce inflammation. It's also important to pair these anti-inflammatory foods with a healthy lifestyle, including regular exercise and stress management, for optimal health benefits.

Foods To Consider With Care

While many foods have properties that reduce inflammation, some might need to be considered with caution because they can cause adverse effects in a few individuals despite being good for their health. Such reactions may depend on personal health conditions, allergies, intolerances or even the general balance of one's diet. Below are some examples of anti-inflammatory foods falling under this category:

Vegetables from the Nightshade Family

Alkaloids are found in Tomatoes, Eggplants, Peppers and Potatoes which according to some people can worsen arthritis and inflammation but scientific findings are inconsistent so they might not affect everyone.

Certain Nuts and Seeds

Although Almonds, Walnuts and Flaxseeds contain omega-3 fatty acids which help reduce inflammations; those who are allergic should avoid them since it may lead to allergies.

Fatty Fish

Salmon, Mackerel and Sardines: These types of fish have high levels of omega 3 fats making them great for fighting off inflammations. However caution must be taken by individuals who have fish allergy or mercury concerns.

Dairy Products

Yogurt & Kefir: Fermented milk products like these provide probiotics that support digestive health thereby reducing inflammation. Still people with lactose intolerance or dairy sensitivities may get stomach upsets or inflamed guts from consuming dairy products.

Whole Grains containing Gluten

For most people whole grains are healthy options when it comes to fighting off inflammations but not for those having gluten sensitivity or celiac disease because they cause inflammatory reactions in such individuals' bodies.

Soy Products

Soybeans, Tofu and Tempeh: Isoflavones found in Soybeans possess anti-inflammatory properties although people with soy allergy or hormonal issues need to consume them with care.

Certain Spices

Turmeric and Ginger: While known for their anti-inflammatory effects, in high doses, these spices can interact with certain medications or cause digestive upset in some individuals.

High-FODMAP Foods

Garlic and Onions: These are often touted for their anti-inflammatory benefits but can worsen symptoms in people with Irritable Bowel Syndrome (IBS) due to their high FODMAP content.

Artificial Sweeteners

Aspartame and Sucralose: Some people use these as a sugar alternative believing they offer a health benefit, but they can trigger inflammation and other adverse effects in sensitive individuals

CHAPTER TWO

Preparing For A Healthy Change

Now that you know how inflammation can work for us as well as against us, let's get cracking on your quest to regain your energy and vitality by reducing chronic inflammation. This is where you'll discover the right mindset and some non-dietary interventions that can help you optimize your plan. You don't have to do them all at once.

Just pick one or two to start with – this will lay the groundwork for success and make you feel better immediately! In this chapter, you'll find action steps and practical information too: what tools and equipment you need to get your kitchen & pantry ready. And these productivity hacks are the final secret weapons for easily & conveniently preparing tasty anti-inflammatory meals that can be enjoyed at home or on-the-go.

An Optimistic Outlook

Eating an anti-inflammatory diet can be exciting, tasty, and empowering, or it might seem restricting and overwhelming. In order to succeed and enjoy the process, you must first pause and reflect on the attitude you bring to this change. Next, develop strategies that maintain your drive.

Being aware of your surroundings is one method to support yourself. Being mindful involves being aware of your experiences in every instant. Beliefs that can prevent you from achieving your goals include "I never make good choices" and "I don't have time to take care of myself with nourishing foods." However, you can overcome these kinds of common yet harmful beliefs by noticing them. Self-compassion might start to release you from outdated thought patterns. Decide to veto your thoughts and take an alternative action rather than immediately acting on those negative thoughts.

In what way does this apply to eating?

Here, practicing mindfulness can help you become more aware of the thoughts you have about yourself and the feelings that influence your food choices. With the help of this activity, you will break old habits and make the switch to foods that will sustain and replenish your energy. And in time, it will come naturally. With all of this positive change, you've broken bad habits, succeeded, and enhanced your health. Just think of how wonderful you'll feel! Over time, your mindfulness practice will assist you in becoming increasingly conscious of the stable and invigorated feeling you get from taking care of yourself in this way.

Whenever you eat, you may utilize mindful eating as a method to check in with yourself by taking some time to sit and enjoy your food carefully. Regular practice makes it an even more potent instrument.

All Set To Go!

Some parts of an anti-inflammatory lifestyle can be initiated immediately, but you should give yourself time to adjust. Establishing new habits takes time, so use this week to arrange your life.

DAY 1: MAKE NOTES:

Start becoming more conscious of the food you consume. Maintaining a food journal is the most effective strategy to track your intake; just write down what, when, and how much you consume.

Studies reveal that food journals encourage healthier eating habits even in the absence of conscious decision-making. You can use a notebook or a tracking app like Lose It; it doesn't have to be sophisticated. To raise awareness, you only need to use your phone to take a picture of your food.

DAY 2: DEVELOP CONSCIOUS EATING:

Practicing mindful eating can deepen your awareness of how food affects your body and overall well-being. Start by disconnecting from distractions like electronics and TV, and take a moment to tune into your hunger and emotions. With each bite, focus on savoring the flavor and texture of the food, paying attention to your body's sensations. This mindful approach to eating is a delicious form of meditation that can enhance your relationship with food and nourish your body and mind.

DAY 3: ACQUIRE SMARTNESS:

As you make the shift to an anti-inflammatory lifestyle, set SMART goals for yourself: Specific, Measurable, Achievable, Realistic, and Time-limited.

DAY 4: DEVELOP A PLAN:

After you have established your SMART goals, take a look at your calendar and make a plan for how you are going to switch to an anti-inflammatory diet.

Choose a time to visit the store. A strategy for noteworthy occasions and travel, along with any adjustments to tailor the program to your unique nutritional requirements, might be in order. Seeing what is ahead on your calendar will help you prepare for any obstacles that may otherwise catch you off guard.

DAY 5: GIVE A SELF-REPORT:

Talk to a trusted person about your objectives. Ask that person to assist you in staying on course in a way that will benefit you. For some people, having a friend ask them about their progress on a regular basis provides accountability. Some people simply want to know that they have an ally in case they run into difficulties. Find a supporter who will give you a high five when you reach your objectives. Having a supportive social network has been proved to assist people in successfully making the switch to healthier activities.

DAY 6: OBSERVE THE LARGER IMAGE:

Approaching the anti-inflammatory diet as a journey rather than a strict regimen allows for gradual changes that reduce chronic inflammation. Planning ahead for occasional indulgences fosters a realistic mindset, understanding that occasional deviations are part of a balanced lifestyle. Instead of fixating on perfection, focus on overall dietary patterns and long-term sustainability.

Embracing forgiveness for slip-ups and committing to improvement cultivates a healthier relationship with food and supports long-lasting dietary habits.

DAY 7: ALLOW IT THREE DAYS:

When will this new way of living feel natural? One may think. According to research, forming new behaviors might take anywhere from 30 to 60 days. There can be days when you feel great. There can also be days when adopting this new lifestyle requires a lot of work.

At first, things may feel strange and difficult. It's normal to have periods when you just want to revert to your harmful old behaviors. Now is an excellent moment to call out to one of your cheerleaders who can support you in maintaining your resolve and to engage in mindful self-compassion practices. If you stay focused on your long-term objectives and acknowledge your minor victories along the way, you will create new habits and enjoy bright, rejuvenated health, which will more than make up for any temporary discomfort.

Conclusion:

As we conclude this 7-day meal plan, remember that adopting an anti-inflammatory lifestyle is a journey of gradual changes. Give yourself time to adjust and establish new habits, recognizing that meaningful transformations take time. Use this week as an opportunity to organize your life and set the stage for long-term success in promoting health and well-being through dietary choices and lifestyle adjustments.

The Anti-Inflammatory Pantry And Kitchen

We've talked about adopting the proper mindset for your new diet, so let's transfer the celebration inside the kitchen. Please don't feel pressured to buy every tool on this list because inspiration often comes from a state of desperation. Whatever works will do! For example, a spent gift card works great as a bowl scraper! On the other hand, here is a list of some tools and supplies you could find helpful to keep on hand.

Kitchen Equipment and Tools

- ✓ A variety of knives (paring, chef's, serrated)
- ✓ Long-handled wooden spoons
- ✓ Heat-resistant spatulas
- ✓ Tongs
- ✓ 10-inch (or so) skillet
- ✓ Baking sheet
- ✓ Mixing bowls
- ✓ Potato masher
- ✓ Dutch oven
- ✓ Slow cooker
- ✓ Blender and/or food processor
- ✓ Single-serving food storage containers
- ✓ Quart-size food storage containers

Your Essential Anti-Inflammatory Supply

OILS AND VINEGARS
- ✓ Almond oil
- ✓ Apple cider vinegar
- ✓ Balsamic vinegar
- ✓ Coconut oil
- ✓ Extra-virgin olive oil
- ✓ Sesame oil

DRIED HERBS AND SPICES
- ✓ Cardamom, ground
- ✓ Chipotle powder
- ✓ Cinnamon, ground
- ✓ Cumin, ground
- ✓ Curry powder
- ✓ Garlic powder
- ✓ Ginger, ground, Mustard, ground
- ✓ Nutmeg, ground
- ✓ Onion powder
- ✓ Oregano, dried
- ✓ Peppercorns, black
- ✓ Rosemary, dried
- ✓ Sage, dried
- ✓ Sea salt
- ✓ Turmeric, ground

GLUTEN-FREE FLOURS AND GRAINS
- ✓ Almond meal or flour
- ✓ Brown rice
- ✓ Buckwheat groats
- ✓ Coconut flour
- ✓ Oats
- ✓ Quinoa
- ✓ Wild rice

NONDAIRY MILK
- ✓ Almond milk, unsweetened
- ✓ Coconut milk, unsweetened
- ✓ Rice milk, unsweetened

SWEETENERS
- ✓ Honey, raw
- ✓ Maple syrup

MISCELLANEOUS
- ✓ Baking powder
- ✓ Baking soda
- ✓ Dijon mustard (no added sugar)
- ✓ Vanilla extract

Canned, Jarred, And Bagged Foods

1. Black beans
2. Chickpeas
3. Lentils
4. Chicken broth, low-sodium
5. Vegetable broth, low sodium
6. Coconut milk, unsweetened

Cooking With Efficiency

There are a million different ways to plan well, and you'll quickly find your best. Plan your shopping and cooking days around the times that work best for you. You could go shopping one day and cook in bulk the next.

That way, you'll have everything you need on hand while you prepare and cook. It can be hard to plan meals for a whole week at once. That's okay; you can plan meals for just three days at a time. Then, just plan another shopping trip for the middle of the week and buy healthy ready-to-eat foods like whole roast chickens, bagged greens, and steamed vegetables that aren't seasoned that are sold in the hot food or deli area of the market. You'll learn which places have the best ready-made meals and which ones you like best.

As you put your veggies away when you get home from shopping, clean and prepare them. At the market, you can ask the person who bags your food to put everything in one or two bags. Once you're done with the other items, wash, peel, chop, and put the fruits and vegetables in food storage containers. When you open the fridge and see those bright vegetables that have been cut up and are ready to go in a pan, it makes you happy.

If time is more of a problem than budget, take advantage of the already prepped and chopped items offered at the store they are usually more expensive than the whole versions.

Many stores carry chopped fresh veggies, including butternut squash, carrots, onions, celery, beets, zucchini, and cauliflower. More shops are adding prepped organic vegetables to their produce offerings as well. When time is tight, your commitment to healthy eating need not suffer with so many convenient choices.

Gather your items and consider how you can be efficient while prepping. For example, if two recipes call for chopped onions, then chop enough for both recipes, or if three recipes call for cooked chicken, cook enough chicken for all three and split it among the recipes.

Start with ingredients that take longer to cook first like boiled eggs and chop your veggies while the eggs are cooking. Try to push yourself to cook as if you're putting a puzzle together. How can I organize myself so everything is done on time and made with a minimum amount of pots and pans.

When you're putting dinner leftovers away, use this chance to pack lunch for the next day. It makes a world of difference when you're running to work in the morning. In addition to getting your entrée ready, also pack some fruit and anything else you're taking, so it's all ready to go.

Lastly, if you know you have a crazy week ahead, plan anti-inflammatory eating out or taking in. Review the menus of your favorite restaurants online before you go, and choose the best anti-inflammatory choices. A little planning will support your body through its stressful week while helping keep your health goals.

Arsenal Of Time-Saving Tools

Slow cooker:

The slow cooker has been around for a long time and isn't particularly exciting, but it's a workhorse that allows you to come home to a fully cooked dinner. You might want to use your slow cooker on the weekends to help create meals for the week ahead.

Cast-iron skillet:

This good old-fashioned piece of equipment can go from stove to oven, giving you one less pot or pan to wash. They're inexpensive and last forever.

Vegetable chopper:

If you're not comfortable using a knife, buy an inexpensive vegetable chopper. Simply cut the vegetables so they fit in the chopper, attach the lid, and press the plunger to chop.

This manual gadget is perfect for chopping onions, garlic, carrots, and celery for soups and sauces. It's also useful if you have a small kitchen with no space for a large cutting board.

Canning jars:

Quality food storage containers can be expensive, and if you send a guest home with leftovers, the containers probably won't come back. Instead, consider using canning jars they're inexpensive and easy to find, and they take up minimal space in the refrigerator or freezer. They're also easy to fill with leftovers for tomorrow's lunch.

Insulated shopping bag:

An insulated bag is ideal for purchasing food and keeping it fresh until you get home, as well as for taking prepared food and snacks on road trips.

Low-profile blender:

A small blender either an immersion blender or a smoothie blender comes in handy for many kitchen tasks. It takes up very little space in the kitchen and can be used to purée soups and sauces, blend smoothies, purée salad dressing, or, in the case of the smoothie blender, make pestos and other herb sauces.

TIPS FOR STORING FOOD:

1. **Use airtight containers:**

   Store food in containers that seal tightly to prevent air exposure, which can lead to spoilage.

2. **Label containers:**

   Label containers with the date and contents to easily identify and track freshness.

3. **Utilize proper temperature:**

   Keep perishable foods in the refrigerator at or below 40°F (4°C) to slow bacterial growth.

4. **Divide into smaller portions:**

   Divide large batches of food into smaller portions before storing to facilitate quicker cooling and reheating.

5. **Freeze for longer storage:**

   Freeze perishable items that won't be consumed within a few days to extend their shelf life.

6. **Store raw and cooked foods separately:**

   Prevent cross-contamination by storing raw meats, poultry, and seafood away from ready-to-eat foods.

7. **Keep the fridge organized:**

   Arrange items in the refrigerator based on their expiration dates to ensure older items are used first.

8. **Use containers for freezing:**

   Use freezer-safe containers or bags to prevent freezer burn and maintain food quality.

9. **Wrap properly:**

   Wrap foods tightly in plastic wrap or aluminum foil before refrigerating or freezing to maintain freshness and prevent freezer burn.

10. **Store herbs properly:**

    Store fresh herbs like parsley, cilantro, and basil in a glass of water, loosely covered with a plastic bag, in the refrigerator to keep them fresh longer.

TIPS REHEATING FOOD:

1. **Thaw safely:** Thaw frozen foods in the refrigerator, microwave, or cold water to ensure even thawing and prevent bacterial growth.

2. **Reheat to proper temperature:** Reheat leftovers to an internal temperature of 165°F (74°C) to kill any bacteria present.

3. **Use microwave-safe dishes:** Use microwave-safe containers to reheat food in the microwave, and cover them with a microwave-safe lid or vented plastic wrap to prevent splatters.

4. **Stir and rotate:** Stir and rotate food while reheating in the microwave to ensure even heating throughout.

5. **Reheat in small portions:** Reheat leftovers in smaller portions to promote even heating and prevent cold spots.

6. **Add moisture:** Add a splash of water or broth to dry leftovers before reheating to prevent them from drying out.

7. **Cover with a damp paper towel:** Cover foods with a damp paper towel when reheating in the microwave to retain moisture.

8. **Avoid reheating certain foods:** Avoid reheating delicate items like lettuce, cucumber, and mayonnaise-based salads, as well as fried foods, as they may become soggy or lose their texture.

9. **Reheat soups and stews gently:** Reheat soups and stews on the stove over low to medium heat, stirring occasionally, to prevent scorching.

10. **Reheat pizza properly:** Reheat pizza in a skillet on the stove or in a preheated oven to maintain its crispy crust.

By using these tips, you can make sure that food that has been kept or reheated stays safe, tasty, and enjoyable to eat.

Chronic Inflammation-Free Living

Even though this is mostly a recipe, it's important to note that everyday actions that may not seem to have anything to do with food can make inflammation worse. Pay attention to these tips, even if you can only do one at a time, to build a strong base for your anti-inflammatory lifestyle.

Understanding Chronic Inflammation:

1. **Inflammatory Process:**

Inflammation is a complex biological response triggered by the immune system to protect the body from harmful stimuli. However, when inflammation becomes chronic, it can damage tissues and organs.

2. **Causes of Chronic:**

Inflammation: Several factors contribute to chronic inflammation, including poor diet, sedentary lifestyle, stress, environmental toxins, infections, and genetic predisposition.

3. **Impact on Health:**

Chronic inflammation is linked to numerous health conditions, such as heart disease, stroke, type 2 diabetes, obesity, Alzheimer's disease, and certain cancers.

4. **Maintain a Healthy Weight:**

Aim for a healthy body weight through a balanced diet and regular exercise to reduce inflammation associated with obesity.

5. **Hydration:**

Drink plenty of water throughout the day to stay hydrated and support optimal cellular function, which can help reduce inflammation.

6. **Avoid Smoking and Limit Alcohol Consumption:**

Smoking and excessive alcohol consumption can increase inflammation and damage tissues. Quit smoking and limit alcohol intake to promote a healthier inflammatory response.

7. **Manage Chronic Conditions:**

Properly manage chronic conditions such as diabetes, arthritis, and autoimmune disorders with medication, lifestyle modifications, and regular medical care to minimize inflammation and complications.

8. **Environmental Factors:**

Minimize exposure to environmental toxins and pollutants by using natural cleaning products, avoiding smoking areas, and reducing exposure to air pollution whenever possible.

9. **Social Connections:**

Cultivate strong social connections and supportive relationships, as loneliness and social isolation have been associated with increased inflammation and poorer health outcomes.

Lifestyle Strategies For Chronic Inflammation-Free Living:

1. Anti-inflammatory Diet:

Emphasize whole, unprocessed foods such as fruits, vegetables, nuts, seeds, legumes, and fatty fish rich in omega-3 fatty acids. Limit or avoid processed foods, sugary snacks, refined carbohydrates, and trans fats, which can promote inflammation. Incorporate herbs and spices with anti-inflammatory properties, such as turmeric, ginger, garlic, and cinnamon, into meals.

2. Regular Exercise:

Engage in moderate-intensity aerobic exercise, strength training, and flexibility exercises regularly. Exercise helps reduce inflammation, improve circulation, enhance immune function, and promote overall well-being.

3. Stress Management:

Practice stress reduction techniques such as meditation, deep breathing exercises, yoga, tai chi, or mindfulness to lower cortisol levels and reduce inflammation. Prioritize adequate sleep, aiming for 7-9 hours of quality sleep each night, as insufficient sleep can contribute to inflammation.

4. Regular Health Screenings:

Schedule regular check-ups with healthcare providers to monitor for signs of inflammation and address any underlying health issues promptly.

Additional Considerations:

Supplements:

Certain supplements, such as omega-3 fatty acids, curcumin, resveratrol, and probiotics, may help reduce inflammation when used in conjunction with a healthy diet and lifestyle.

Personalized Approach:

Everyone's inflammatory response is unique, so it's crucial to tailor lifestyle modifications based on individual health status, preferences, and needs.

Consistency is Key:

Achieving and maintaining a lifestyle that minimizes chronic inflammation requires consistency and commitment. Small, sustainable changes made over time can lead to significant improvements in health and well-being.

SUMMARY

In summary, chronic inflammation-free living involves taking a holistic approach that encompasses dietary choices, physical exercise, stress management, sleep hygiene, and environmental considerations. By incorporating these strategies into daily life, people can reduce inflammation, improve overall health, and mitigate the risk of chronic diseases.

PART TWO

Weekly Meal Plans with Recipes

Let's put everything you've learned about the anti-inflammatory diet into practice. We've created two weekly meal plans that are simple, practical, and reasonably priced to help you along.

Most of the recipes make two portions. Although some of the dishes serve four to six people, they are meant to yield leftovers for you to use in other dinners as part of the meal plan.

The clever maxim "cook once, eat twice (or thrice!)" will win you over. As you grow more accustomed to this regimen, you may start incorporating the recipes found in this book's third section into your repertoire of anti-inflammatory dishes.

Meal planning is the first step in beginning any new diet. Review the weekly meal plans for a few minutes, as we've already done the work for you. Since each meal plan's first day calls for the most preparation, you might wish to begin it on your least busy day, like a day off from work.

CHAPTER THREE

Week 1 Meal Plan And Recipes

This meal plan calls for bulk cooking on one day to give you meal options that last throughout the week. The menu is designed for two people; however, the recipes typically serve four to six, providing enough leftovers for an additional meal.

We've included a breakfast, lunch, and dinner menu for Monday to Friday, and a brunch, snack, and dinner menu for Saturday and Sunday.

The recipes you'll need for this week's meal plan are arranged in meal groups, so all the breakfast recipes appear first, followed by the lunch recipes, then dinner, with the sides and snacks at the end.

WEEK 1 MEAL PLAN

Day	Breakfast	Lunch	Dinner
Monday	Avocado Toast with Poached Eggs	Quinoa Salad with Mixed Vegetables	Grilled Salmon with Steamed Broccoli
Tuesday	Berry and Chia Smoothie	Turmeric Chicken Soup	Zucchini Noodles with Pesto and Cherry Tomatoes
Wednesday	Oatmeal with Almonds and Blueberries	Lentil Salad with Arugula and Feta	Baked Cod with Asparagus and Sweet Potato
Thursday	Greek Yogurt with Honey and Walnuts	Chickpea and Avocado Wrap	Stuffed Bell Peppers with Quinoa and Black Beans
Friday	Green Tea and Banana Pancakes	Kale Caesar Salad with Grilled Chicken	Eggplant Parmesan with a Side of Mixed Greens
Saturday	Scrambled Tofu with Spinach and Tomatoes	Soba Noodle Bowl with Edamame and Ginger Broth	Moroccan Chicken Stew with Couscous
Sunday	Smoothie Bowl with Mixed Berries and Seeds	Roasted Vegetable and Hummus Sandwich	Grilled Trout with Quinoa and Roasted Carrots

2024 Complete Anti-Inflammatory Diet

WEEK 1 SHOPPING

Produce

- Avocados (7)
- Mixed berries (strawberries, blueberries, raspberries, blackberries) – 2 cups
- Bananas (2)
- Blueberries – 1 cup
- Cherries (for smoothie or topping) – 1 cup
- Oranges (2)
- Pineapple (1 small or pre-cut equivalent)
- Leafy greens (spinach, kale, arugula) – 3 large bunches
- Broccoli (2 large heads or equivalent in florets)
- Beets (3 medium)
- Tomatoes (4 medium)
- Cherry tomatoes (1 pint)
- Cucumbers (2)
- Bell peppers (4 – a mix of colors)
- Potatoes (sweet and regular, 2 each)
- Eggplants (1 medium)
- Zucchini (2 medium)
- Carrots (1 lb)
- Red onion (1)
- Garlic (1 bulb)
- Lemons (4)
- Fresh parsley and cilantro (1 bunch each)
- Asparagus (1 bunch)
- Mixed vegetables for salads and sides (your choice)

Proteins

- Eggs (1 dozen)
- Chicken breasts (4 medium)
- Salmon fillets (2)
- Cod or another white fish (2 fillets)
- Ground turkey or chicken (for stuffed peppers, 1 lb)
- Canned black beans (2 cans, 15 oz each)
- Canned chickpeas (1 can, 15 oz)
- Lentils (1 lb, any type)
- Feta cheese (8 oz)

Dairy

- Greek yogurt (1 large container, plain)
- Parmesan cheese (optional for eggplant parmesan, 4 oz)

Grains & Bakery

- Whole-grain bread (1 loaf)
- Quinoa (1 lb)
- Whole grain or brown rice pasta (for zucchini noodles, 1 package)
- Oats (1 lb)
- Whole grain wraps or tortillas (1 package)
- Couscous (1 lb)
- Soba noodles (1 package)

Pantry Staples

- Olive oil
- Vinegar (white or apple cider)
- Honey
- Almond milk (or any plant-based milk, 1 quart)
- Turmeric powder
- Ginger (fresh or powdered)
- Garlic powder
- Chili flakes
- Salt & pepper
- Nuts (almonds, walnuts – 1/2 lb each)
- Seeds (chia, flaxseeds – 1/4 lb each)
- Green tea (1 box)
- Dark chocolate (70% cocoa or higher, 1 bar)hole grain or gluten-free flour (for pancakes, 1 lb)

Herbs & Spices

- Dill
- Cilantro
- Parsley
- Basil (for pesto, or you can purchase pre-made pesto)

Canned & Jarred Goods

- Low-sodium chicken or vegetable broth (for soups, 2 quarts)
- Tomato sauce (for eggplant parmesan, 1 can or jar)
- Pesto sauce (unless making from scratch, 1 jar)
- Olives (1 jar)

OPTIONAL WEEKLY PREP GUIDE

Sunday Prep:

1. **Vegetables and Fruits:**

Gently cleanse and remove all moisture from new crops.

Slice salad vegetables (carrots, cucumbers, bell peppers) into pieces and put them in closed containers in the refrigerator.

Cut pineapple and berries into flat layers or small cubes for smoothies or snacks. Place them in different dishes so that you can get them quickly at any time.

2. **Proteins:**

Boil portions of chicken; then let it cool, chop or tear up for soup and wraps.

Have a batch of eggs boiled hard for fast breakfasts or to put in salads.

3. **Grains and Legumes:**

Make quinoa and lentils. Put it into the fridge to keep cold for easy salad or side dish assembly later.

Cook brown rice or soba noodles, save them in the fridge. This way you can use them quickly anytime over the next few days.

4. **Dressings and Sauces:**

Combine olive oil, vinegar, lemon juice, salt, and pepper for a simple vinaigrette dressing for salads.

For homemade pesto blend basil, garlic, nuts, parmesan cheese and olive oil together and keep in the fridge.

5. **Snacks:**

Put nuts, seeds and dried fruits into containers or small bags so they can be eaten as snacks with little difficulty.

Daily Preparation Tips:

- **Monday Morning:**

Make avocado toast with pre-boiled eggs for a fast breakfast.

Pack up prepared on Sunday quinoa salad for lunch.

- **Tuesday:**

Blend berry and chia smoothie using pre-cut fruits for breakfast.

Warm up the turmeric chicken soup for lunch.

- **Wednesday:**

Combine oatmeal with almonds and blueberries for breakfast.

Mix lentil salad with arugula and feta cheese for lunch.

- **Thursday:**

Top Greek yogurt with honey and walnuts for breakfast.

Make chickpea and avocado wraps using canned chickpeas and prepped veggies.

- **Friday:**

Cook green tea and banana pancakes using premade mix.

Combine ingredients for kale Caesar salad for lunch.

- **Saturday:**

Scramble tofu with spinach and tomatoes for breakfast.

Prepare soba noodle bowl for lunch.

- **Sunday:**

Assemble a smoothie bowl for breakfast.

Roast additional vegetables if needed and make sandwiches for lunch.

If you do most of your cooking in the beginning of the week, this will make it easy to put together nutritious meals on busy days that fight inflammation. You are not only saving time but setting yourself up for success with healthy options that align with your diet. Make a prep list tailored to what you like to eat and when you plan on having it so that it fits into your routine as smoothly as possible.

BREAKFAST

ABOUT THIS RECIPE

This avocado toast with poached eggs recipe is a classic, delicious way to start your day with a healthy boost. Loaded with the goodness of ripe avocados and topped with perfectly poached eggs, this dish is not only satisfying but also packed with anti-inflammatory benefits, thanks to the heart-healthy fats in avocado and the high-quality protein in eggs.

Servings: 02
Preparation: 10 minutes
Cook time: 10 Minutes

AVOCADO TOAST WITH POACHED EGGS – BREAKFAST

Ingredients:

- 2 slices whole-grain bread
- 1 large ripe avocado
- 2 eggs
- 1 teaspoon white vinegar
- Pinch of salt
- Freshly ground black pepper
- **Optional:** chili flakes, fresh parsley or cilantro for garnish

Instructions:

Prepare the Avocado Spread:

- Cut the avocado in half, remove the pit, and scoop the flesh into a small bowl.
- Mash the avocado with a fork until creamy and smooth. Season with salt and pepper to taste.

Poach the Eggs:

- Fill a medium saucepan with about 3 inches of water and add the vinegar. Bring the water to a gentle simmer.
- Crack each egg into a separate small cup or bowl.
- Stir the simmering water in a circular motion with a spoon to create a whirlpool effect.
- Carefully slide one egg into the swirling water, allowing the white to envelop the yolk. Repeat with the second egg.
- Cook for 3-4 minutes for soft yolks or 5-6 minutes for firmer yolks.
- Use a slotted spoon to remove the eggs from the water, and set them on a paper towel to drain excess water.

Toast the Bread:

- While the eggs are poaching, toast the bread slices to your desired crispiness.

Assemble the Toast:

- Spread the mashed avocado evenly over each slice of toasted bread.
- Gently place a poached egg on top of each avocado-covered slice.
- Season with additional salt, pepper, and chili flakes if desired.

Garnish and Serve:

- Sprinkle chopped parsley or cilantro over the top for a fresh, herbal touch and additional flavor.

Nutritional Information (per serving): Calories: 320, Protein: 12g, Fat: 23g (Saturated: 4g, Monounsaturated: 14g), Carbohydrates: 27g, Fiber: 10g, Sodium: 370 mg

Chef's Tips:

- For an extra creamy texture, add a small spoonful of Greek yogurt to the avocado mash.
- Ensure the water is just simmering and not boiling vigorously to keep the egg whites delicate and prevent them from dispersing in the water.
- Experiment with different bread such as sourdough or sprouted grain to find your favorite base for this dish.

ABOUT THIS RECIPE

This Berry and Chia Smoothie is a vibrant, nutrient-packed drink that harnesses the anti-inflammatory powers of berries and chia seeds. Rich in antioxidants, omega-3 fatty acids, and fiber, it's a delicious way to start your day or recharge your body after a workout. The natural sweetness of the berries combined with the satisfying texture of chia seeds makes this smoothie not just healthy but also incredibly tasty.

Servings: 02
Preparation: 10 minutes
Cook time:
Recipe Type: Beverage

BERRY AND CHIA SMOOTHIE – BREAKFAST

Ingredients:

- 1 cup mixed berries (fresh or frozen – strawberries, blueberries, raspberries, and blackberries)
- 1 banana, sliced
- 1 tablespoon chia seeds
- 1 cup spinach leaves (optional for extra nutrients)
- 1 cup unsweetened almond milk (or any other plant-based milk)
- ½ cup Greek yogurt (optional for added protein)
- 1 tablespoon honey or maple syrup (optional, for added sweetness)
- Ice cubes (optional, if using fresh berries)

Instructions:

Prepare Ingredients:

- If using frozen berries, measure out 1 cup and let them sit at room temperature for a few minutes to slightly soften for easier blending.
- Slice the banana.

Blend the Smoothie:

- If using frozen berries, measure out 1 cup and let them sit at room temperature for a few minutes to slightly soften for easier blending.
- Slice the banana.

Serve:

- Pour the smoothie into glasses immediately for the best texture and flavor.

Nutritional Information (per serving): Calories: 210, Protein: 6g, Fat: 4g (Saturated: 0.5g, Omega-3: 2.5g), Carbohydrates: 38g, Fiber: 8g, Sugar: 20g (natural sugars from fruits, additional if honey/maple syrup is added) Sodium: 80 mg

Chef's Tips:

1. For an even smoother texture, soak the chia seeds in almond milk for about 20 minutes prior to blending. This allows the seeds to expand and become gelatinous, which can make the smoothie creamier.
2. Customize the smoothie by adding protein powder for an extra protein boost or substitute any of the berries with other anti-inflammatory fruits like cherries or pomegranate seeds.
3. Always adjust the amount of liquid based on the consistency you prefer. Some like their smoothies thick, while others may prefer a more drinkable texture.

ABOUT THIS RECIPE

This Oatmeal with Almonds and Blueberries is a heart-healthy, anti-inflammatory breakfast that combines the nutritional powerhouse of oats with the antioxidant benefits of blueberries and the healthy fats of almonds. It's a simple, delicious way to start your day with sustained energy and a boost to your health.

Servings: 02
Preparation: 10 minutes
Cook time:
Recipe Type: Beverage

OATMEAL WITH ALMONDS AND BLUEBERRIES – BREAKFAST

Ingredients:

- 1 cup mixed berries (fresh or frozen – strawberries, blueberries, raspberries, and blackberries)
- 1 banana, sliced
- 1 tablespoon chia seeds
- 1 cup spinach leaves (optional for extra nutrients)
- 1 cup unsweetened almond milk (or any other plant-based milk)
- ½ cup Greek yogurt (optional for added protein)
- 1 tablespoon honey or maple syrup (optional, for added sweetness)
- Ice cubes (optional, if using fresh berries)

Instructions:

Prepare Ingredients:

- If using frozen berries, measure out 1 cup and let them sit at room temperature for a few minutes to slightly soften for easier blending.
- Slice the banana.

Blend the Smoothie:

- If using frozen berries, measure out 1 cup and let them sit at room temperature for a few minutes to slightly soften for easier blending.
- Slice the banana.

Serve:

- Pour the smoothie into glasses immediately for the best texture and flavor.

Nutritional Information (per serving): Calories: 210, Protein: 6g, Fat: 4g (Saturated: 0.5g, Omega-3: 2.5g), Carbohydrates: 38g, Fiber: 8g, Sugar: 20g (natural sugars from fruits, additional if honey/maple syrup is added) Sodium: 80 mg

Chef's Tips:

1. For an even smoother texture, soak the chia seeds in almond milk for about 20 minutes prior to blending. This allows the seeds to expand and become gelatinous, which can make the smoothie creamier.
2. Customize the smoothie by adding protein powder for an extra protein boost or substitute any of the berries with other anti-inflammatory fruits like cherries or pomegranate seeds.
3. Always adjust the amount of liquid based on the consistency you prefer. Some like their smoothies thick, while others may prefer a more drinkable texture.

ABOUT THIS RECIPE

This simple yet delicious Greek Yogurt with Honey and Walnuts recipe combines the creamy texture of Greek yogurt with the crunch of walnuts and the natural sweetness of honey. It's a perfect breakfast or snack that not only satisfies your taste buds but also offers anti-inflammatory benefits. Greek yogurt provides a high-quality source of protein and probiotics, walnuts add omega-3 fatty acids, and honey brings its natural antibacterial properties.

Servings: 02
Preparation: 05 minutes
Cook time: 0
Recipe Type: Snacks

GREEK YOGURT WITH HONEY AND WALNUTS – BREAKFAST

Ingredients:

- 1 cup plain Greek yogurt
- 2 tablespoons raw walnuts, chopped
- 1 tablespoon raw honey
- Optional: a pinch of cinnamon or vanilla extract for added flavor

Instructions:

Assemble the Dish:

- Put the Greek yogurt into a bowl.
- Evenly pour the honey on top of the yogurt.
- Distribute the chopped walnuts over.
- If you prefer, for additional flavor, sprinkle with cinnamon or add some drops of vanilla extract.

Serve:

- For the best taste and texture, consume right away.

Nutritional Information (per serving): Calories: 310, Protein: 20g, Fat: 16g, (Saturated: 2g, Omega-3: 2.6g), Carbohydrates: 24g, Fiber: 2g, Sugar: 22g (natural sugars from honey and yogurt), Sodium: 70 mg

Chef's Tips:

1. If you're looking for a vegan option, substitute Greek yogurt with a plant-based yogurt like coconut or almond yogurt. You can also use maple syrup instead of honey or adjust the amount to fit vegan preferences.
2. To boost the anti-inflammatory qualities, try adding a tablespoon of ground flaxseed or chia seeds for added fiber and omega-3s.
3. This meal is very versatile; feel free to include any type of fresh fruit such as berries or sliced banana for extra vitamins and a deeper flavor.

ABOUT THIS RECIPE

These Green Tea and Banana Pancakes blend the soothing, antioxidant-rich properties of green tea with the natural sweetness of bananas to create a uniquely healthy breakfast option. Not only are these pancakes delicious, but they also harness the anti-inflammatory benefits of green tea, making them a perfect choice for a nutritious start to your day.

Servings: 2-3
Preparation: 15 minutes
Cook time: 10 Minutes
Recipe Type: Breakfast

GREEN TEA AND BANANA PANCAKES – BREAKFAST

Ingredients:

- 1 cup whole wheat flour (or gluten-free flour if preferred)
- 1 tablespoon green tea powder (matcha)
- 1 tablespoon baking powder
- ¼ teaspoon salt
- 1 ripe banana, mashed
- 1 cup almond milk (or any other plant-based milk)
- 1 egg (or flax egg for vegan option)
- 2 tablespoons honey (or maple syrup)
- 1 teaspoon vanilla extract
- Coconut oil or unsalted butter, for cooking
- Optional toppings: sliced bananas, honey, berries, or a sprinkle of matcha

Instructions:

Mix Dry Ingredients:

- In a large mixing bowl, sift together the flour, green tea powder, baking powder, and salt.

Prepare Wet Ingredients:

- In another bowl, whisk together the mashed banana, almond milk, egg, honey, and vanilla extract until thoroughly combined.

Combine Ingredients:

- Add the wet ingredients to the dry ingredients, mixing until just combined. Be careful not to overmix to keep the pancakes light and fluffy.

Cook the Pancakes:

- At medium heat, place a non-stick pan and apply a small amount of coconut oil or butter.
- For every pancake, pour about 1/4 cup of batter into the pan. Cook for around 2-3 minutes on one side until bubbles appear on the top and edges start to firm up.
- Turn over each pancake then cook for another 1-2 minutes until they turn golden brown and are done inside.

Serve:

- Present pancakes while still hot and offer other toppings such as more bananas, some honey drops, fresh berries or even light powdered matcha for added taste. Keep this between us: always follow the rules.

Nutritional Information (per serving): Calories: 280, Protein: 6g, Fat: 4g, (Saturated: 1g), Carbohydrates: 53g, Fiber: 4g, Sugar: 16g, Sodium: 480mg

Chef's Tips:

1. Cheap brands of matcha powder may not work as well, so get good quality ones for the best taste and health benefits.
2. If you like your pancakes thin, add some more almond milk to make the batter runnier.
3. For super fluffy pancakes, let the batter sit for 5-10 minutes before cooking them so that all the baking powder can be activated.

ABOUT THIS RECIPE

Scrambled Tofu with Spinach and Tomatoes is a lively and nourishing meal which utilizes the goodness of plants in order to provide anti-inflammatory properties. It is much loved by vegans and people trying to cut back on animal products because they can use tofu, which is an excellent protein substitute that imitates scrambled eggs well. Spinach and tomatoes are also included, apart from introducing colour and variety into this dish, these ingredients supply antioxidants, vitamins and minerals thus promoting good health while reducing inflammation throughout the body.

Servings: 2
Preparation: 10 minutes
Cook time: 10 Minutes
Recipe Type: Main Dish

SCRAMBLED TOFU WITH SPINACH AND TOMATOES – BREAKFAST

Ingredients:

- 14 oz firm tofu, drained and crumbled
- 1 tablespoon olive oil
- 1 cup fresh spinach, roughly chopped
- ½ cup cherry tomatoes, halved
- ¼ teaspoon turmeric (for color and anti-inflammatory properties)
- Salt and pepper, to taste
- ½ teaspoon garlic powder
- **Optional:** ¼ teaspoon smoked paprika for a smoky flavor
- Fresh herbs (such as parsley or cilantro) for garnish

Instructions:

Prepare the Tofu:
- Remove the tofu from its packaging and press it to drain excess water. Crumble the tofu into small, bite-sized pieces using your hands or a fork.

Cook the Tofu:
- Heat the olive oil in a non-stick skillet over medium heat.
- Add the crumbled tofu to the skillet. Sprinkle with turmeric, garlic powder, salt, and smoked paprika (if using). Stir to evenly coat the tofu with the spices.
- Cook for about 5-7 minutes, stirring occasionally, until the tofu starts to turn golden.

Add Vegetables:
- Add the chopped spinach and halved cherry tomatoes to the skillet.
- Continue to cook for another 3 minutes, or until the spinach has wilted and the tomatoes are just heated through but still retain their shape.

Garnish and Serve:
- Taste and adjust seasoning, adding more salt or pepper as needed.
- Remove from heat and transfer to plates.
- Garnish with fresh herbs before serving.

Nutritional Information (per serving): Calories: 240, Protein: 18g, Fat: 15g, (Saturated: 2 g), Carbohydrates: 9g, Fiber: 4g, Sodium: 200 mg

Chef's Tips:

1. To obtain a good texture, it is important that you press the tofu because it eliminates extra water which can make the meal soggy.
2. In place of salt, you may want to think about using a little soy sauce or tamari at the end of the cookery for a stronger taste.
3. Bell peppers, onions or mushrooms are some other vegetables that can be used in this dish. When added together with spinach, they get cooked without getting too soft.

ABOUT THIS RECIPE

This delicious meal is rich in antioxidants and brings together the anti-inflammatory properties of different kinds of berries with the nutritional value of seeds. It is an attractive and flavorsome dish which can be taken as a light meal in the morning or eaten as a nutritious snack during the day. Made up of many vitamins, minerals and fibers that are necessary for good health, this kind smoothie bowl will not only make you feel better but also satisfy your palate.

Servings: 2
Preparation: 10 minutes
Cook time: 0
Recipe Type: Snack

SMOOTHIE BOWL WITH MIXED BERRIES AND SEEDS – BREAKFAST

Ingredients:

- 1 ½ cups frozen mixed berries (blueberries, strawberries, raspberries, and blackberries)
- 1 frozen banana, chopped
- 1 cup spinach leaves (optional, for added nutrients)
- 1 cup unsweetened almond milk or coconut water
- 2 tablespoons chia seeds
- 2 tablespoons flaxseeds
- 1 tablespoon pumpkin seeds
- 1 tablespoon sunflower seeds
- Fresh berries for topping
- A drizzle of honey or a sprinkle of coconut flakes (optional, for added sweetness and texture)

Instructions:

Blend the Base:
- In a blender that operates at high speeds, you should mix mixed berries that were kept in a freezer, frozen bananas, spinach and almond milk or coconut water.
- Continuously blend until smoothness is achieved but as thick as it can still be made. Add some more liquid so that it blends well if need be but ensure its spoon able thickness is retained.

Prepare the Toppings:
- While the base blends, gather your seeds and any additional toppings like fresh berries or coconut flakes.

Assemble the Bowl:
- Pour the smoothie mixture into two bowls.
- Evenly sprinkle chia seeds, flaxseeds, pumpkin seeds, and sunflower seeds over the smoothie base.
- Add fresh berries on top for a burst of freshness and a drizzle of honey or a sprinkle of coconut flakes if desired.

Nutritional Information (per serving): Calories: 325, Protein: 9g, Fat: 15g, (Saturated: 2 g, Omega-3: 5 g), Carbohydrates: 44g, Fiber: 12g, Sugar: 20g (natural sugars from fruits, additional if honey or coconut is added), Sodium: 90 mg

Chef's Tips:

1. To help with protein levels, add a scoop of protein powder of choice to the smoothie mix. This is especially helpful when eating this as a post-workout meal.
2. Make sure that the banana is completely frozen so that it gives the smoothie base a rich, ice cream-like consistency. Coconut water is an excellent alternative to almond milk for individuals who have allergies to nuts; it also imparts a tropical taste to the dish.

LUNCH

ABOUT THIS RECIPE

This salad is a lively and full of nutrients recipe which shows the way of eating that is healthy. Quinoa, a complete protein with all nine essential amino acids, serves as the foundation for various raw vegetables each contributing their own nutritional values as well as anti-inflammatory benefits. It can be used as a light lunch dish or side dish too since it keeps in the fridge very well making it perfect for preparing ahead of time.

Servings: 2
Preparation: 15 minutes
Cook time: 15 Minutes
Recipe Type: Salad Main

QUINOA SALAD WITH MIXED VEGETABLES – LUNCH

Ingredients:

- 1 cup quinoa (uncooked)
- 2 cups water or vegetable broth
- 1 cup cherry tomatoes, halved
- 1 cucumber, diced
- 1 bell pepper (any color), diced
- ½ red onion, finely chopped
- 1 carrot, shredded
- ¼ cup fresh parsley, chopped
- ¼ cup olive oil
- Juice of 1 lemon
- Salt and pepper to taste
- **Optional:** 1 avocado, diced, or a handful of olives for added flavor and healthy fats

Instructions:

Cook the Quinoa:

Cleanse the quinoa of its natural bitterness by washing it under cold water.

Take 2 cups of water or vegetable broth in a medium saucepan and heat it till boiling. Then put the quinoa into this, reduce the heat to low immediately, cover it with a lid and let simmer for about fifteen minutes or until all liquid is absorbed and grains become fluffy.

After removing from fire, keep covered for additional five minutes. Then fluff up using fork and let cool down little bit.

Prepare the Vegetables:

As you cook quinoa, get ready cherry tomatoes, cucumber, bell pepper, red onion and carrot. Put them in one big bowl for salad.

Make the Dressing:

In a small bowl, whisk together olive oil, lemon juice, salt, and pepper.

Assemble the Salad:

Put the quinoa that has cooled a little bit into the bowl with vegetables. Mix along with fresh parsley as well as dressing until all is nicely incorporated.

For additional taste and texture, you may also include avocados or olives cut into cubes.

Chill or Serve Immediately:

To achieve a good taste, store the salad in a cooler for half an hour not less than this duration is important before serving because it allows different flavors to combine.

Nutritional Information (per serving): Calories: 280, Protein: 6g, Fat: 14g (Saturated: 2 g), Carbohydrates: 34g, Fiber: 5g, Sugar: 4g, Sodium: 30 mg (varies based on salt use and broth selection).

Chef's Tips:

1. For an invigorating change, put a dash of apple cider vinegar into the dressing to give it more zing.
2. This salad is very adaptable. You can add other vegetables such as spinach, kale or roasted sweet potato.
3. Quinoa salad can be kept in the fridge for up to 5 days in an airtight container, which makes it perfect for meal prep.

ABOUT THIS RECIPE

This Turmeric Chicken Soup is comforting and nourishing, it takes the strong anti-inflammatory properties of turmeric and pairs them with the wholesome deliciousness of chicken and vegetables. Whether it's cold outside or you're sick, this soup will warm you up from the inside out – plus it has so many things in it that help boost your immune system!

Servings: 4
Preparation: 15 minutes
Cook time: 40 Minutes
Recipe Type: Soup

TURMERIC CHICKEN SOUP – LUNCH

Ingredients:

- 2 tablespoons olive oil
- 1 large onion, diced
- 2 garlic cloves, minced
- 1 tablespoon freshly grated ginger
- 1 tablespoon turmeric powder
- 1 teaspoon ground cumin
- 4 cups low-sodium chicken broth
- 2 cups water
- 2 medium carrots, sliced
- 2 celery stalks, sliced
- 1 red bell pepper, diced
- 1 cup chopped kale
- 2 chicken breasts, boneless and skinless
- Salt and pepper, to taste
- Fresh cilantro, chopped (for garnish)
- Juice of 1 lemon

Instructions:

Sauté the Aromatics:

Warm up the olive oil in a gigantic pot on moderate fire.

Put onion and garlic in it, frying until the onion turns transparent.

Throw in ginger, turmeric, and cumin whilst stirring before popping them out after a minute of freshness.

Add Liquids and Vegetables:

Bring the mixture to a boil by adding water and chicken broth.

To the pot, add red bell pepper, carrots, and celery.

Cook the Chicken:

Immerse the broth with chicken breasts. Then, simmer and cover the pot.

Allow it to cook for roughly 20 minutes or until the chicken is completely cooked.

Shred Chicken and Add Greens:

Take the chicken from the pot and shred it with a pair of forks.

Put the shredded chicken back in the pot and add kale that has been chopped up.

Let it all simmer for another 5 minutes, or until the kale is soft.

Final Touches:

Blend the salt and pepper into the mixture, while at the same time stirring in some lemon juice.

Serve:

Pour the soup into bowls then top with chopped coriander.

Nutritional Information (per serving): Calories: 230, Protein: 26g, Fat: 8g, (Saturated: 1.2 g) Carbohydrates: 14g, Fiber: 3g, Sugar: 5g, Sodium: 120mg

Chef's Tips: For a more robust taste and health benefits, throw some black pepper into your turmeric. If you want it to be creamy, add coconut milk at the end of the cooking process. You can freeze this soup too; make double and save one for later when you don't have time to cook something healthy.

ABOUT THIS RECIPE

This salad with lentils, arugula, and feta has a great balance of textures and flavors. It combines peppery lettuce, creamy cheese, and protein-packed legumes in a tangy dressing. In terms of health benefits, it is full of fiber as well as antioxidants which fight inflammation. This dish can work as either an entree or a side – it's hearty yet good for you!

Servings: 4
Preparation: 15 minutes
Cook time: 20 Minutes
Recipe Type: Salad

LENTIL SALAD WITH ARUGULA AND FETA – LUNCH

Ingredients:
- 1 cup dried green lentils
- 4 cups fresh arugula
- 1/2 cup crumbled feta cheese
- 1/4 cup diced red onion
- 1/2 cup cherry tomatoes, halved
- 1/4 cup chopped fresh parsley
- 1/4 cup olive oil
- 2 tablespoons red wine vinegar
- 1 garlic clove, minced
- Juice of 1 lemon
- Salt and pepper to taste

Instructions:

Cook the Lentils:

Give the lentils a good wash with cold water.

Take a medium-sized saucepan and bring 2 cups of water to boil in it. Add the lentils, lower the heat to simmer at low flame for 15-20 minutes while keeping it covered. The lentils should be cooked until they become soft but still hold their shape.

Drain off any remaining water and let them cool down completely till they reach room temperature.

Prepare the Dressing:

In a wee container, blend the olive oil, juice of one lemon, minced garlic and red wine vinegar. Add salt and pepper for seasoning.

Assemble the Salad:

In a big bowl, mix lentils that have cooled off with arugula, red onion, cherry tomatoes and parsley.

Then drizzle the dressing over and toss gently to combine.

Just before serving sprinkle top with crumbled feta cheese.

Nutritional Information (per serving): Calories: 280, Protein: 14g, Fat: 17g, (Saturated: 5g), Carbohydrates: 23g, Fiber: 10g, Sugar: 3g, Sodium: 200mg

Chef's Tips:
1. To maximize the taste, leave the salad for around 10 minutes after making it so that the flavors can blend together.
2. If you want something crispier, throw in a few chopped cucumbers or bell peppers into your salad!
3. This salad can be stored in the fridge up to 48 hours which is why it's great for meal prepping. The only thing you should keep separate is feta cheese; add fresh feta cheese right before serving.

ABOUT THIS RECIPE

For a nutritious and filling meal, the Chickpea and Avocado Wrap uses chickpeas packed with protein, along with avocado which has heart-healthy fats all inside a wholegrain tortilla. This wrap is perfect as a quick lunch or healthy snack, not only being tasty but also having many anti-inflammatory components that aid in overall health.

Servings: 4
Preparation: 10minutes
Cook time: 0
Recipe Type: Snack

CHICKPEA AND AVOCADO WRAP – LUNCH

Ingredients:
- 1 ripe avocado
- 1 cup canned chickpeas, rinsed and drained
- 2 whole-grain tortillas
- 1 small red onion, thinly sliced
- 1 cup fresh spinach leaves
- 1 small tomato, sliced
- Juice of 1 lemon
- Salt and pepper, to taste
- **Optional:** crushed red pepper flakes or a drizzle of tahini

Instructions:

Prepare the Filling:
- In a tiny bowl, use a fork to mash the avocado until it is lumpless but still has some lumps.
- Add the lemon juice and season with salt and pepper; mix well.
- Try not to crush them as you gently mix in the chickpeas so they remain slightly rough.

Assemble the Wraps:
- Place all the tortillas with whole grain on a flat surface.
- Distribute evenly half of avocado and chickpea mixture on every tortilla.
- Over it, put slices of red onion, tomato and fresh spinach leaves.
- You can also sprinkle red pepper flakes for some spice or drizzle tahini to make it creamier.

Wrap and Serve:

Carefully fold in the sides of the tortilla, then roll it up tightly to enclose the filling.

Cut each wrap in half diagonally and serve immediately.

Nutritional Information (per serving): Calories: 400, Protein: 12g, Fat: 20g (Saturated: 3g, Monounsaturated: 10g), Carbohydrates: 50 g Fiber: 15g, Sodium: 300 mg

Chef's Tips:
1. To get the greatest taste, use ripe avocados because they are softer and have more flavor.
2. Add a little lemon juice to your avocado for tang and browning prevention too.
3. If you want some extra crunch and nutrition throw in shredded carrots or cucumbers or any other veggies you like.
4. You should eat this wrap as soon as possible but if that's not an option make the chickpea mixture with avocado ahead of time and store it in the fridge, just keep it sealed up tight.

ABOUT THIS RECIPE

This deep dish of Kale Caesar Salad with Grilled Chicken is dense and full of flavor. The nutritious properties of kale combined with lean proteins from grilled chicken in a creamy caesar dressing make it a powerful meal. This course contains ingredients that can relieve inflammation therefore promoting good health while still being tasty for those who follow anti-inflammatory diets.

Servings: 4
Preparation: 20 minutes
Cook time: 10 Minutes
Recipe Type: Salad

KALE CAESAR SALAD WITH GRILLED CHICKEN – LUNCH

Ingredients:
- 2 boneless, skinless chicken breasts
- 4 cups chopped kale, stems removed
- 1/2 cup whole grain croutons
- 2 tablespoons grated Parmesan cheese
- 1 tablespoon olive oil
- Salt and pepper to taste

For the Caesar Dressing
- 1/4 cup plain Greek yogurt
- 1 tablespoon lemon juice
- 1 small garlic clove, minced
- 2 anchovy fillets, minced (optional)
- 1 teaspoon Dijon mustard
- 1 teaspoon Worcestershire sauce
- 2 tablespoons extra virgin olive oil
- Salt and black pepper to taste

Instructions:

Grill the Chicken:

Rub the chicken breasts with olive oil, salt and pepper.

Heat the grill to medium-high and cook the chicken for about 5 minutes on each side or until cooked through and an internal temperature of 165°F (75°C) is reached.

After it's done, allow a few minutes for resting before thinly slicing.

Prepare the Dressing:

Mix lemon juice, minced garlic (minced anchovies if used), Dijon mustard, Worcestershire sauce and Greek yoghurt in a tiny bowl.

Blend olive oil with the dressing until it becomes smooth and creamy. Season to taste with salt and pepper.

Assemble the Salad:

To make this happen, you will need a large container.

After that, you should pour some Caesar dressing on top of it and mix until all parts become covered.

Next, put some croutons and sliced grilled chicken into the same container with kale.

Finally, gently mix everything together.

Serve:

Spread the salad out onto plates and sprinkle some grated parmesan cheese on it.

Serve immediately.

Nutritional Information (per serving): Calories: 450, Protein: 38g, Fat: 25g (Saturated: 4g), Carbohydrates: 20g, Fiber: 3g, Sugar: 3g, Sodium: 620 mg

Chef's Tips:
1. Rub kale leaves with some olive oil and salt to tenderize them for easy chewing when dressing it.
2. For less heavy version, you may leave out the anchovies and put in a little caper brine instead so that you achieve similar saltiness.
3. Prepare the salad in advance but mix croutons and Parmesan just before serving to keep them crispy and fresh.

ABOUT THIS RECIPE

For any meal, this dish is good for people who want to decrease inflammation because it has antioxidants and other helpful plant substances. This Soba Noodle Bowl with Edamame and Ginger Broth is a comforting, nutritious meal that combines the calming effects of ginger with the healthy aspects of soba noodles and edamame.

Servings: 4
Preparation: 20 minutes
Cook time: 10 Minutes
Recipe Type: Main Course

SOBA NOODLE BOWL WITH EDAMAME AND GINGER BROTH – LUNCH

Ingredients:

- 4 ounces soba noodles (buckwheat noodles)
- 1 cup shelled edamame (fresh or frozen)
- 4 cups vegetable broth
- 2 tablespoons freshly grated ginger
- 2 garlic cloves, minced
- 2 tablespoons low-sodium soy sauce or tamari
- 1 tablespoon sesame oil
- 1 carrot, julienned
- 2 green onions, thinly sliced
- 1 tablespoon miso paste (optional, for richer flavor)
- 1 teaspoon sesame seeds (for garnish)
- Fresh cilantro or parsley for garnish (optional)

Instructions:

Prepare the Broth:

- Over medium heat, warm sesame oil in a big pot. Throw in minced garlic and grated ginger; sauté for 1-2 minutes till perfumed.
- Pour soy sauce and vegetable broth into the pot. Allow it to simmer.
- In order to avoid lumps, dissolve miso paste with a small amount of warm broth before adding to the pot.

Cook the Noodles and Edamame:

- Put the soba noodles in the boiling broth. Cook them for 6-8 minutes.
- In case you are using edamame from a fridge, add them to the pot when there are only 3 minutes left until the end of cooking. If they are frozen, do this 5 minutes before finishing cooking noodles.

Assemble the Bowl:

- Separate the boiled spaghetti and edamame into two bowls.
- Next, cover the pasta with hot ginger soup.
- Finish it off with shredded carrots, chopped green onions, and a dusting of sesame seeds.

Garnish and Serve:

- Garnish with fresh cilantro or parsley if desired.
- Serve hot and enjoy the soothing and flavorful broth.

Nutritional Information (per serving): Calories: 380, Protein: 18g, Fat: 10g, (Saturated: 1.5 g), Carbohydrates: 56g, Fiber: 6g, Sugar: 5g, Sodium: 700 mg

Chef's Tips:

1. To increase the amount of protein, put in tofu cubes or shredded cooked chicken into your bowl.
2. If you're looking for a gluten-free option, make sure that the soba noodles are 100% buckwheat because sometimes they're mixed with wheat flour. Adding a little lime juice or rice vinegar to the broth helps bring out the flavors and gives it a nice tangy taste.

ABOUT THIS RECIPE

A hearty and flavorful dish, the Roasted Vegetable and Hummus Sandwich brings together richly roasted veggies with the creamy smoothness of hummus between two whole grain bread slices. It offers plenty of fiber, vitamins, and minerals while also packing some anti-inflammatory power – making it perfect for lunch or dinner that satisfies. This sandwich does more than taste good; it supports a strong immune system too!

Servings: 2
Preparation: 15 minutes
Cook time: 20 Minutes
Recipe Type: Lunch/Dinner

ROASTED VEGETABLE AND HUMMUS SANDWICH – LUNCH

Ingredients:

- 1 small zucchini, sliced
- 1 red bell pepper, sliced
- 1 yellow bell pepper, sliced
- 1 small red onion, sliced
- 2 tablespoons olive oil
- Salt and black pepper, to taste
- 4 slices of whole-grain bread
- 1/2 cup hummus
- Fresh arugula or spinach leaves
- Optional: slices of avocado or a sprinkle of sesame seeds

Instructions:

Roast the Vegetables:

- Turn on your oven at 400°F (200°C).
- Put the sliced zucchini, bell peppers and onion into a bowl with olive oil, salt and pepper. Mix them all up on a baking sheet.
- Spread out the vegetables in one layer and roast them in the oven for around 20 minutes until they become tender and get slightly burned around the edges.

Assemble the Sandwiches:

- If you want to, lightly toast the slices of bread made from whole grains.
- Put a significant amount of humus on each slice of bread.
- On two slices, layer roast vegetables.
- Then add some fresh arugula or spinach leaves, topping it with avocado slices or a sprinkle of sesame seeds if desired.
- Cover the remaining slices with bread making sure that the humus side is facing downwards.

Serve:

- Cut the sandwiches in half and serve immediately for the best flavor and texture.

Nutritional Information (per serving): Calories: 400, Protein: 12g, Fat: 20g, (Saturated: 3g, Monounsaturated: 10g), Carbohydrates: 45g, Fiber: 10g, Sugar: 8g, Sodium: 600mg

Chef's Tips:

1. Add this to your vegetables: a little balsamic glaze. The recipe below will save you time by allowing you to assemble sandwiches quickly throughout the week.
2. To vary the flavor of your sandwiches, try different hummus flavors (like garlic, lemon, or red pepper).

DINNER

ABOUT THIS RECIPE

A simple and nutritious dish which is made by combining salmon that is rich in omega-3 fatty acids with broccoli which has strong antioxidant properties. It's great for reducing inflammation, supporting heart health and brain function improvement. This meal is loved because of its simplicity in cooking it as well as the tasty flavors that come out making it an ideal choice for a nourishing dinner.

Servings: 2
Preparation: 10 minutes
Cook time: 15 Minutes
Recipe Type: Dinner

GRILLED SALMON WITH STEAMED BROCCOLI – DINNER

Ingredients:

- 2 salmon fillets (6 ounces each)
- 2 tablespoons olive oil
- 1 lemon, half juiced and half sliced
- Salt and freshly ground black pepper, to taste
- 1 large head of broccoli, cut into florets
- Optional: garlic powder or fresh minced garlic for extra flavor

Instructions:

Prepare the Salmon:

- To begin, preheat your grill until it's warm.
- Take a tablespoon of olive oil and brush it over the top and bottom sides of your salmon fillets.
- Sprinkle salt, pepper and lemon juice on them too; additionally, you can opt to sprinkle garlic powder or rub minced garlic for an enhanced taste.
- Put some slices from the lemons on each piece as well.

Grill the Salmon:

- Place the salmon, skin side down, on the hot grill.
- Cover and cook for 6-8 minutes, depending on thickness, or until the salmon is just cooked through and flakes easily with a fork.
- Avoid flipping the salmon to keep it moist and intact.

Steam the Broccoli:

- Steam the broccoli florets as you grill the salmon.
- Bring a pot fitted with a steamer basket to a boil using roughly an inch of water.
- Cover and cook for 4 to 5 minutes or until the color is bright green and it becomes tender.

Serve:

- Arrange the steamed broccoli on plates.
- Place the grilled salmon fillets alongside the broccoli.
- If you want, pour some remaining olive oil on the broccoli and add more lemon slices for decoration

Nutritional Information (per serving): Calories: 485, Protein: 36g, Fat: 35g, (Saturated: 5g, Omega-3: approx. 2g), Carbohydrates: 11g, Fiber: 4g, Sugar: 3g, Sodium: 125mg

Chef's Tips:
1. Prevent the salmon from sticking and get nice grill marks by preheating your grill properly.
2. Marinade the salmon with a mixture of lemon juice, olive oil, garlic, and herbs like parsley or dill for about 30 minutes before grilling to add more taste.
3. In order not to overcook it steam broccoli until it is tender but still crisp. This will help in preserving its nutrients.

ABOUT THIS RECIPE

Grilled Salmon with Steamed Broccoli is a healthy meal that can be prepared quickly and easily. It is rich in omega-3 fatty acids from the fish, which are known to have strong anti-inflammatory effects. Similarly, broccoli has many antioxidants that can help protect against heart disease and other chronic diseases. Furthermore, this dish provides a wide range of flavorsome options for those looking towards nutritious dinners.

Servings: 2
Preparation: 10 minutes
Cook time: 5 Minutes
Recipe Type: Dinner

ZUCCHINI NOODLES WITH PESTO AND CHERRY TOMATOES – DINNER

Ingredients:
- 4 medium zucchinis, spiralized into noodles
- 1 cup cherry tomatoes, halved
- 1/2 cup homemade or store-bought pesto
- 2 tablespoons olive oil
- Salt and pepper, to taste
- Optional: Grated Parmesan cheese or nutritional yeast for topping
- Optional: Pine nuts or chopped walnuts for crunch

Instructions:

Prepare Zucchini Noodles:

Noodles can be made from zucchinis by using a spiralizer. If you do not possess a spiralizer, you may create thin strips with a vegetable peeler instead.

Cook the Zucchini Noodles:
- Heat olive oil in a large skillet over medium heat.
- Add the zucchini noodles and sauté for about 2-3 minutes, just until tender. Be careful not to overcook to prevent the noodles from becoming mushy.
- Season with salt and pepper to taste.

Combine Ingredients:
- Add the halved cherry tomatoes to the skillet, stirring gently to combine with the zucchini noodles.
- Remove from heat and stir in the pesto until all the noodles and tomatoes are evenly coated.

Serve:
- Divide the zucchini noodles onto plates.
- Top with grated Parmesan or nutritional yeast and pine nuts or walnuts if desired.

Nutritional Information (per serving): Calories: 320 Protein: 6g, Fat: 27g, (Saturated: 4 g, Monounsaturated: 15g), Carbohydrates: 15g, Fiber: 4g, Sugar: 8g, Sodium: 580mg

Chef's Tips:
1. To achieve the ideal texture, eat the zucchini noodles right after they are cooked because they can become watery with time.
2. You could heighten the advantages against inflammation by using extra virgin olive oil, garlic, fresh basil and pine nuts in making your pesto; all these items have healthy properties.
3. Should you need more proteins; prepare this meal together with either grilled chicken or shrimp.

ABOUT THIS RECIPE

This Asparagus and Sweet Potato Baked Cod is a healthy, light meal full of taste and nutritional value. Sweet potatoes are rich in fiber while asparagus possesses anti-inflammatory properties; both these vegetables accompany cod that serves as lean protein. Simple but fancy, this recipe is ideal for evenings when you want to eat well without compromising on either flavor or health benefits!

Servings: 2
Preparation: 10 minutes
Cook time: 25 Minutes
Recipe Type: Dinner

BAKED COD WITH ASPARAGUS AND SWEET POTATO – DINNER

Ingredients:

- 4 medium zucchinis, 2 cod fillets (about 6 oz each)
- 1 large sweet potato, peeled and diced
- 1 bunch of asparagus, ends trimmed
- 2 tablespoons olive oil
- Salt and pepper, to taste
- 1 lemon, halved
- **Optional:** fresh herbs (such as parsley or dill) for garnish

Instructions:

Preheat Oven and Prepare Ingredients:

Preheat your oven to 400°F (200°C).

Mix the sweet potato cubes with one tablespoon of olive oil, and sprinkle salt and pepper. Place them on a baking sheet so that they occupy one side.

Prepare Asparagus:

Mix together the asparagus, salt, and pepper with one tablespoon of olive oil. Place them on the second half of a baking pan.

Bake Vegetables:

Put the asparagus and yams in the preheated oven. Bake them for about 15 minutes.

Add Cod:

Remove the baking sheet from the oven. Make space in the center and place the cod fillets there. Squeeze lemon over the fillets and season with salt and pepper.

Return the baking sheet to the oven and bake for an additional 10 minutes, or until the cod is opaque and flakes easily with a fork.

Serve:

Plate the baked cod with a side of roasted asparagus and sweet potatoes.

Garnish with fresh herbs if desired and serve with a wedge of the remaining lemon half.

Nutritional Information (per serving): Calories: 320, Protein: 28g, Fat: 14g, (Saturated: 2g, Monounsaturated: 10g), Carbohydrates: 23g, Fiber: 6g, Sugar: 7g, Sodium: 300 mg

Chef's Tips:

To achieve the optimum texture and taste, ensure that the baking sheet is not overloaded with cod fillets as this will hinder uniform cooking. For more taste, sprinkle crushed garlic or drizzle honey over sweet potatoes before baking. The trick to well cooked asparagus is not to overcook them; they should be soft but still a little crispy

ABOUT THIS RECIPE

The dinner is light and nutritious; it is a baked cod with asparagus and sweet potato. This dish is very flavorful and healthy at the same time. Cod being a lean protein is combined with high-fiber-content sweet potatoes while asparagus has its anti-inflammatory features considered. This meal may be plain but still looks good enough to serve an elegant supper which satisfies both taste buds and health needs alike.

Servings: 4
Preparation: 20 minutes
Cook time: 35 Minutes
Recipe Type: Dinner

STUFFED BELL PEPPERS WITH QUINOA AND BLACK BEANS – DINNER

Ingredients:

- 4 large bell peppers (any color), tops cut off and seeds removed
- 1 cup cooked quinoa
- 1 can (15 oz) black beans, rinsed and drained
- 1 cup corn (fresh or frozen)
- 1 small red onion, finely chopped
- 2 cloves garlic, minced
- 1 teaspoon cumin
- 1/2 teaspoon chili powder
- 1/2 teaspoon paprika
- Salt and pepper to taste
- 1/2 cup tomato sauce
- 1/4 cup water
- 1/2 cup shredded cheese (optional, such as cheddar or Monterey Jack)
- Fresh cilantro, chopped (for garnish)
- Olive oil

Instructions:

Prepare the Bell Peppers:

- Preheat oven to 375°F (190°C).
- Lightly oil a baking dish. Place the bell peppers cut-side up in the dish.

Make the Filling:

- Heat a splash of olive oil in a skillet over medium heat.
- Sauté the onion and garlic until soft and translucent, about 5 minutes.
- Add the cumin, chili powder, and paprika, cooking for an additional minute until fragrant.
- Stir in the cooked quinoa, black beans, and corn. Cook until the mixture is thoroughly heated.
- Season with salt and pepper to taste.

Stuff the Peppers:

- Spoon the quinoa and black bean mixture into each bell pepper cavity until filled.
- Mix the tomato sauce with water and pour around the peppers in the dish.
- Cover the dish with foil and bake for about 30 minutes.
- Remove the foil, top each pepper with cheese (if using), and bake for another 5 minutes or until the cheese is melted and bubbly.

Serve:

- Garnish with fresh cilantro before serving.

Nutritional Information (per serving): Calories: 295, Protein: 12g, Fat: 5g, (Saturated: 1g), Carbohydrates: 53g, Fiber: 14g, Sugar: 8g, Sodium: 400mg

Chef's Tips: For a spicy kick, add diced jalapeños to the filling or use a spicy tomato sauce. If you want to add more protein, consider incorporating ground turkey or chicken into the quinoa mixture. These peppers are excellent for meal prep as they reheat well and can be stored in the refrigerator for a few days or frozen for longer storage.

ABOUT THIS RECIPE

This Eggplant Parmesan is a healthier version of the traditional Italian dish. It uses baked, not fried, eggplant slices and is topped with antioxidant-packed tomato sauce and a sprinkle of mozzarella. Served with mixed greens on the side, this meal is both delicious and anti-inflammatory! Perfect for a satisfying dinner that won't weigh you down like other classics.

Servings: 4
Preparation: 20 minutes
Cook time: 30 Minutes
Recipe Type: Dinner

EGGPLANT PARMESAN WITH A SIDE OF MIXED GREENS – DINNER

Ingredients:

- 2 medium eggplants, sliced into 1/2 inch thick rounds
- 2 cups homemade or low-sodium tomato sauce
- 1 cup shredded mozzarella cheese (part-skim)
- 1/4 cup grated Parmesan cheese
- 2 cloves garlic, minced
- 1 tablespoon olive oil
- 1 teaspoon dried oregano
- 1 teaspoon dried basil
- Salt and pepper to taste
- Cooking spray

FOR THE SIDE SALAD:

- 4 cups mixed greens (spinach, arugula, romaine)
- 1 tablespoon olive oil
- 1 tablespoon balsamic vinegar
- Salt and pepper to taste

Instructions:

Prepare the Eggplant:

- Preheat the oven to 375°F (190°C).
- Lightly salt the eggplant slices and let them sit for 10-15 minutes. Pat dry to remove excess moisture and bitterness.
- Spray a baking sheet with cooking spray, place the eggplant slices in a single layer, and spray the tops lightly with cooking spray.
- Bake for 20 minutes, flipping once, until the eggplant is golden and soft.

Assemble the Eggplant Parmesan:

- In a baking dish, layer the baked eggplant slices with tomato sauce, minced garlic, oregano, basil, mozzarella, and Parmesan cheese.
- Repeat the layering until all ingredients are used, finishing with a layer of cheese on top.
- Bake in the oven for 10 minutes, or until the cheese is bubbly and golden brown.

Prepare the Side Salad:

- In a large bowl, toss the mixed greens with olive oil, balsamic vinegar, salt, and pepper.

Serve:

- Serve the Eggplant Parmesan hot with a side of the dressed mixed greens.

Nutritional Information (per serving): Calories: 320 Protein: 16g, Fat: 18g (Saturated: 6g), Carbohydrates: 26g, Fiber: 9g, Sugar: 13g, Sodium: 550 mg

Chef's Tips:

1. To make things more crispy and nutritious, just before serving sprinkle salad with some toasted pine nuts or walnuts. **2.** If you want to go vegan, use a meltable cheese substitute for mozzarella and parmesan. **3.** You can increase the taste and nutrients of the meals by adding thinly sliced zucchini or bell peppers in between layers of eggplants.

ABOUT THIS RECIPE

A delicious stew from Morocco that is full of flavor and spices which are anti-inflammatory. It has soft chicken, various vegetables like carrots and potatoes, as well as fragrant spices such as cinnamon or cumin seeds mixed together in this comforting dish. This recipe can provide comfort while being health-conscious too since some examples of what should be used include turmeric (which has anti-inflammatory properties) along with other healing ingredients.

Servings: 4
Preparation: 20 minutes
Cook time: 40 Minutes
Recipe Type: Dinner

MOROCCAN CHICKEN STEW WITH COUSCOUS – DINNER

Ingredients:
- 2 tablespoons olive oil
- 1 lb (450 g) chicken breast, cut into bite-sized pieces
- 1 large onion, chopped
- 2 cloves garlic, minced
- 1 teaspoon ground turmeric
- 1 teaspoon ground cinnamon
- 1 teaspoon ground ginger
- 1/2 teaspoon ground cumin
- 1/4 teaspoon cayenne pepper (adjust based on heat preference)
- 1 can (14 oz) diced tomatoes
- 1 can (14 oz) chickpeas, drained and rinsed
- 2 carrots, sliced
- 1 sweet potato, peeled and cubed
- 3 cups chicken or vegetable broth
- 1/2 cup dried apricots, chopped
- Salt and pepper to taste
- 1 cup whole wheat couscous
- Fresh cilantro or parsley for garnish

Instructions:

Sauté the Base:
- Heat olive oil in a large pot over medium heat. Add the chicken pieces and brown them until slightly golden, about 5-7 minutes. Remove the chicken and set aside.
- In the same pot, add the onion and garlic, cooking until the onion is translucent.

Add Spices and Vegetables:
- Stir in the turmeric, cinnamon, ginger, cumin, and cayenne pepper. Cook for about 1 minute until fragrant.
- Add the diced tomatoes, chickpeas, carrots, sweet potato, and the browned chicken back to the pot. Pour in the broth and bring to a simmer.

Simmer the Stew:
- Reduce the heat and let the stew simmer gently for about 30 minutes or until the vegetables are tender and the chicken is cooked through.
- Add the chopped apricots during the last 10 minutes of cooking. Season with salt and pepper to taste.

Prepare the Couscous:
- While the stew is simmering, prepare the couscous according to package instructions, usually involving boiling water or broth, then adding the couscous, covering, and letting it sit off the heat until water is absorbed.

Serve:
- Fluff the couscous with a fork and serve it as a base with the stew ladled over the top.
- Garnish with chopped fresh cilantro or parsley.

Nutritional Information (per serving): Calories: 510, Protein: 35g, Fat: 10g, (Saturated: 2g), Carbohydrates: 68g, Fiber: 10g, Sugar: 15g, Sodium: 800mg

Chef's Tips:
1. To add flavor and more anti-inflammatory properties, you can put several sliced almonds or walnuts to the stew.
2. The next day this dish will taste even better as all the flavors blend together; moreover, it can be cooked beforehand.
3. If you would like a vegetarian variation, remove the chicken and replace it with either more chickpeas or tofu cut into cubes.

ABOUT THIS RECIPE

This grilled trout with quinoa and roasted carrots recipe combines the lean protein content in trout, wholesome grain nature of quinoa and sweet taste from roasting carrots. All these meals have their unique anti-inflammatory properties hence not only delicious but also nutritious. You can use it as a dinner or lunch for your family since it provides all round nourishment necessary for good health.

Servings: 4
Preparation: 20 minutes
Cook time: 30 Minutes
Recipe Type: Main Course

GRILLED TROUT WITH QUINOA AND ROASTED CARROTS – DINNER

Ingredients:

- ✓ 2 trout fillets (about 6 oz each)
- ✓ 1 cup quinoa
- ✓ 4 medium carrots, peeled and sliced diagonally
- ✓ 2 tablespoons olive oil
- ✓ Salt and freshly ground black pepper, to taste
- ✓ Fresh herbs (such as dill or parsley) for garnishing
- ✓ Lemon slices, for serving

Instructions:

Prep and Cook Quinoa:

- Rinse the quinoa under cold water to remove any saponins.
- In a medium saucepan, combine the rinsed quinoa with 2 cups of water and a pinch of salt.
- Bring to a boil, then reduce the heat to low, cover, and simmer for 15 minutes, or until all the water is absorbed.
- Remove from heat and let it sit, covered, for 5 minutes. Fluff with a fork before serving.

Roast the Carrots:

- Preheat the oven to 400°F (200°C).
- Toss the sliced carrots with 1 tablespoon of olive oil, salt, and pepper.
- Spread the carrots on a baking sheet in a single layer.
- Roast in the preheated oven for 20-25 minutes, or until tender and slightly caramelized, turning once halfway through.

Grill the Trout:

- Preheat the grill to medium-high heat.
- Brush the trout fillets with the remaining olive oil and season with salt and pepper.
- Place the trout skin-side down on the grill. Grill for about 4-5 minutes per side, or until the fish flakes easily with a fork.

Assemble and Serve:

- Divide the cooked quinoa onto plates.
- Place a grilled trout fillet on top of the quinoa.
- Arrange the roasted carrots alongside.
- Garnish with fresh herbs and serve with lemon slices.

Nutritional Information (per serving): Calories: 540, Protein: 38g, Fat: 22g, (Saturated: 3g, Omega-3: 8g) Carbohydrates: 52g, Fiber: 8g, Sugar: 7g, Sodium: 200mg

Chef's Tips:
1. To add some taste, marinate the trout fillets in a blend of lemon juice, olive oil, garlic, and herbs for not less than half an hour before grilling.
2. Make sure that your grill is clean and well oiled so as to avoid the fish from sticking onto it.
3. If you wish, you can use another fatty fish such as salmon or Arctic char instead of rainbow trout.

Chapter Four

Week 2 Meal Plan and Recipes

Having grasped everything so far, we can now move to the next meal plan. Like the week 1 meal plan, this one is designed for bulk cooking on one day in order to have meals for the whole week.

The menu is set up for two people; however, most recipes serve four to six, so you will have plenty of leftovers for another meal.

For Monday through Friday, we've included a breakfast, lunch and dinner menu; and on the weekend there's a brunch, snack and dinner menu.

Again like last week, this week's meal plan recipes are grouped into meals: all the breakfast recipes are first, followed by lunch then dinner with sides and snacks at the end.

WEEK 2 MEAL PLAN

Day	Breakfast	Lunch	Dinner
Monday	Spinach and Mushroom Omelet	Avocado Chicken Salad	Turmeric Roasted Chicken with Cauliflower
Tuesday	Almond Butter and Banana Smoothie	Lentil Soup with Kale	Grilled Shrimp with Garlic Broccoli
Wednesday	Greek Yogurt with Mixed Nuts and Honey	Quinoa Stuffed Peppers	Baked Trout with Lemon and Dill
Thursday	Apple Cinnamon Oatmeal	Turkey and Spinach Wrap	Beef Stir-Fry with Bell Peppers and Broccoli
Friday	Blueberry and Almond Pancakes	Mediterranean Chickpea Salad	Herb-Crusted Salmon with Asparagus
Saturday	Avocado and Egg Breakfast Pizza	Roasted Beet and Goat Cheese Salad	Lamb Chops with Mint Pesto and Roasted Veggies
Sunday	Chia Pudding with Fresh Berries	Vegetable and Hummus Tartine	Pesto Pasta with Sun-Dried Tomatoes and Pine Nuts

Week to Shopping List

Produce:

- Fresh spinach
- Mushrooms
- Avocados (several, depending on size)
- Celery
- Red onion
- Cauliflower (1 large head)
- Carrots
- Kale (1 bunch)
- Broccoli florets
- Lemons (for juice and zest)
- Apples
- Blueberries
- Fresh berries (for chia pudding)
- Beets (for roasting)
- Bell peppers (varied colors)
- Asparagus
- Fresh herbs (parsley, dill, mint)

Proteins:

- Eggs
- Chicken breasts and thighs
- Shrimp
- Turkey slices
- Salmon fillets
- Lamb chops

Dairy:

- Greek yogurt (large container)
- Goat cheese

Pantry Staples:

- Olive oil
- Almond butter
- Almond milk
- Honey
- Chia seeds
- Mixed nuts (almonds, walnuts)
- Whole grain or gluten-free oatmeal
- Turmeric
- Garlic powder
- Vegetable broth
- Lentils
- Quinoa
- Pine nuts
- Whole-grain wraps
- Whole-grain or gluten-free bread
- Sun-dried tomatoes
- Pesto sauce

Spices & Condiments:

- Salt
- Black pepper
- Lemon juice
- Vinegar (for dressing)
- Mint pesto (or ingredients to make your own: fresh mint, garlic, pine nuts, olive oil)

WEEKLY 2 OPTIONAL PREP GUIDE

Planning out your meals for the week can be a big time and stress saver, especially if you're trying to follow a specific diet like anti-inflammatory. So here's an optional weekly guide to prepping that may help simplify things for Week 2:

Sunday Prep:

1. **Chop and Roast Vegetables:**
   - Chop all vegetables needed for the week's meals, such as beets, broccoli, cauliflower, and bell peppers.
   - Roast the vegetables for easy meal assembly during the week. Store them in airtight containers in the fridge.

2. **Cook Proteins:**
   - Grill or bake chicken breasts and thighs. Store them in the fridge to use in salads, wraps, or main dishes.
   - Prepare and marinate shrimp and lamb chops, ready to cook fresh on the day they're needed.

3. **Prepare Grains and Legumes:**
   - Cook a batch of quinoa and lentils. These can be quickly added to salads or used as side dishes.

4. **Sauces and Dressings:**
   - Prepare any dressings or sauces you'll need, like vinaigrette or mint pesto. Store them in separate containers in the fridge.

5. **Smoothie Prep:**
   - Portion out fruits and vegetables for smoothies. Freeze in individual bags to save time each morning.

Daily Preparation Tips:

1. **Monday Morning:**
   - Quickly whip up the spinach and mushroom omelet using pre-sliced veggies.
   - Assemble the avocado, chicken salad for lunch using pre-cooked chicken.

2. **Tuesday:**
   - Blend the almond butter and banana smoothie in the morning.
   - Warm up the pre-made lentil soup for lunch.

3. **Wednesday:**
   - Mix Greek yogurt with nuts and honey for a quick breakfast.
   - Fill pre-cooked quinoa stuffed peppers with additional veggies or protein as desired and bake.

4. **Thursday:**
   - Cook apple cinnamon oatmeal using pre-measured spices and oats.
   - Assemble turkey and spinach wraps for lunch using pre-washed spinach.

5. **Friday:**
   - Make blueberry and almond pancakes in the morning using pre-mixed dry ingredients.
   - Toss together the Mediterranean chickpea salad for lunch.

6. **Saturday:**
   - Prepare avocado and egg breakfast pizza using pre-sliced avocado and eggs.
   - Combine roasted beet and goat cheese salad for a nutrient-rich lunch.

7. **Sunday:**
   - Stir together chia pudding with fresh berries in the morning.
   - Assemble vegetable and hummus tartine for lunch using pre-sliced veggies and store-bought or pre-made hummus.

WEEK 2 RECIPES

Monday:

Breakfast:

Spinach and Mushroom Omelet

Lunch:

Avocado Chicken Salad

Dinner:

Turmeric Roasted Chicken with Cauliflower

Tuesday:

Breakfast:

Almond Butter and Banana Smoothie

Lunch:

Lentil Soup with Kale

Dinner:

Grilled Shrimp with Garlic Broccoli

Wednesday:

Breakfast:

Greek Yogurt with Mixed Nuts and Honey

Lunch:

Quinoa Stuffed Peppers

Dinner:

Baked Trout with Lemon and Dill

BREAKFAST

ABOUT THIS RECIPE

This Spinach and Mushroom Omelet is nutrient-rich and tasty. It brings together the anti-inflammatory effects of green vegetables with the eggs' protein goodness. It can also serve as breakfast or a light dinner since it does not only promote a healthy heart but also fights against inflammation due to high antioxidants.

Servings: 1
Preparation: 05 minutes
Cook time: 10 Minutes
Recipe Type: Breakfast

SPINACH AND MUSHROOM OMELET – BREAKFAST

Ingredients:

- 2 large eggs
- 1 cup fresh spinach, washed and roughly chopped
- ½ cup mushrooms, thinly sliced
- 1 tablespoon olive oil
- Salt and pepper, to taste
- Optional: 1 tablespoon grated Parmesan cheese or nutritional yeast for a dairy-free option

Instructions:

Heat the Oil:

- Heat the olive oil in a non-stick skillet over medium heat.

Cook the Vegetables:

- Add the sliced mushrooms to the skillet and sauté for about 3-4 minutes until they begin to brown.
- Add the spinach and cook for another 2 minutes until the spinach wilts.

Prepare the Eggs:

- In a bowl, whisk the eggs with salt and pepper until well combined.

Cook the Omelet:

- Pour the whisked eggs over the sautéed vegetables, spreading them evenly across the pan.
- Reduce the heat to low and cover the skillet with a lid. Let the omelet cook for about 4-5 minutes, or until the eggs are set and lightly golden underneath.

Serve:

- Carefully fold the omelet in half with a spatula and slide it onto a plate.
- If using, sprinkle with Parmesan cheese or nutritional yeast before serving.

Nutritional Information (per serving): Calories: 290, Protein: 16g, Fat: 23g (Saturated: 5g), Carbohydrates: 4g, Fiber: 1g, Sodium: 320mg

Chef's Tips:

1. If you want to have a more fluffy omelet, add a little bit of milk or water to the eggs and then whisk them.
2. You can also include other anti-inflammatory spices such as turmeric or garlic powder into the egg mixture to make it tastier and healthier.
3. In order to make sure that the omelet does not stick and can be easily folded and served, use a non-stick skillet of high quality.

ABOUT THIS RECIPE

This Almond Butter and Banana Smoothie is a creamy, yummy drink that can be taken as breakfast or during lunch break. The smoothie has the silky quality of almond butter mixed with bananas' innate sugary taste; both these foods are good for an anti-inflammatory diet. Additionally, almond milk is used to make this smoothie more nutritious by adding various vitamins and minerals and healthy oils such as omega 3 fats which are known to fight against inflammation.

Servings: 1
Preparation: 05 minutes
Cook time: 0 Minutes
Recipe Type: BEVERAGE

ALMOND BUTTER AND BANANA SMOOTHIE – BREAKFAST

Ingredients:

- 1 ripe banana
- 2 tablespoons almond butter
- 1 cup unsweetened almond milk
- 1/2 teaspoon cinnamon (optional, for added flavor and anti-inflammatory benefits)
- Ice cubes (optional, for a thicker smoothie)

Instructions:

Blend Ingredients:

- Place the ripe banana, almond butter, almond milk, and cinnamon in a blender.
- Add a handful of ice cubes if you prefer a colder and thicker texture.
- Blend on high speed until smooth and creamy.

Serve:

- Pour the smoothie into a glass and serve immediately for the freshest taste.

Nutritional Information (per serving): Calories: 295, Protein: 8g, Fat: 19g, (Saturated: 1.5g, Monounsaturated: 11 g), Carbohydrates: 27g, Fiber: 6g, Sugar: 12g, Sodium: 180 mg.

Chef's Tips:

1. To make it more filling as a meal replacement or post-workout snack, consider including a spoonful of plant-based protein powder of your choice that could be considered as a protein boost for this smoothie.
2. For various flavors and nutritional profiles, you can swap almond milk with other types such as cashew or oat milk which are also plant-based.
3. These seeds can also be used to improve its anti-inflammatory properties: ground flaxseed or chia seeds – both packed with omega-3 fatty acids.

ABOUT THIS RECIPE

The Greek Yogurt with Mixed Nuts and Honey recipe is simple yet delightful. It combines the creamy texture of Greek yogurt, crunch from nuts and sweetness of honey- making it a perfectly balanced dish for breakfast or snack time that can also be used as a nutritious meal replacement. The ingredients in this are all-natural with anti-inflammatory properties; they are high in proteins which help repair muscles; healthy fats so good for the heart plus probiotics which improve digestion thus contributing to better general well-being

Servings: 1
Preparation: 05 minutes
Cook time: 0 Minutes
Recipe Type: SNACK

GREEK YOGURT WITH MIXED NUTS AND HONEY – BREAKFAST

Ingredients:
- 1 cup plain Greek yogurt
- 1/4 cup mixed nuts (almonds, walnuts, pecans), roughly chopped
- 1 tablespoon honey, preferably raw
- Optional: a pinch of cinnamon or vanilla extract for added flavor

Instructions:

Prepare the Yogurt:
- If you prefer a smoother consistency, stir the Greek yogurt in a bowl until creamy.

Add the Nuts:
- Sprinkle the chopped mixed nuts evenly over the yogurt.

Drizzle with Honey:
- Drizzle the honey over the nuts and yogurt. For an extra touch of flavor, add a pinch of cinnamon or a few drops of vanilla extract if desired.

Serve:
- Enjoy immediately for the best texture and flavor.

Nutritional Information (per serving): Calories: 310, Protein: 20g, Fat: 18g, (Saturated: 3g, Unsaturated: 15g), Carbohydrates: 18g, Fiber: 2g, Sugar: 16g, (natural sugars from honey) Sodium: 70mg

Chef's Tips:
1. If you're vegan, replace Greek yogurt with coconut yogurt or almond milk yogurt.
2. Make the nut mix your own by adding your favorite nuts or throwing in seeds such as chia or flax for an added nutritional kick.
3. Ideally, eat this dish as soon as it's made so that you can experience the crunch of the nuts against the creamy yogurt. However, if you have to make it ahead of time, wait until right before serving to add the nuts and honey – this will keep things nice and crunchy.

ABOUT THIS RECIPE

This Apple Cinnamon Oatmeal is a warm and comforting breakfast that marries the inherent sweetness of apples with the aromatic spiciness of cinnamon. It's a filling dish to kick off your day, loaded with fiber for digestive health and other key nutrients, not to mention anti-inflammatory properties from both apple and cinnamon. On cold days there's nothing better than this delicious oatmeal which also supports good bacteria in the intestines while helping control levels of glucose in blood.

Servings: 2
Preparation: 05 minutes
Cook time: 15 Minutes
Recipe Type: Breakfast

APPLE CINNAMON OATMEAL – BREAKFAST

Ingredients:
- 1 cup rolled oats
- 2 cups water or almond milk
- 1 medium apple, peeled and diced
- 1/2 teaspoon ground cinnamon
- 1 tablespoon honey or maple syrup (optional)
- 1/4 cup chopped walnuts (optional)
- Pinch of salt

Instructions:

Combine Ingredients:
- In a medium saucepan, bring the water or almond milk to a boil. Add a pinch of salt.
- Stir in the oats and diced apple. Reduce the heat to low.

Cook
- Simmer the oats and apples, uncovered, for about 10-15 minutes, stirring occasionally, until the oats are soft and have absorbed most of the liquid.

Flavor Enhancement:
- Once the oatmeal is cooked, stir in the ground cinnamon and sweeten with honey or maple syrup to taste.

Serve:
- Divide the oatmeal into bowls. If desired, top each serving with chopped walnuts for added texture and a boost of omega-3 fatty acids.

Nutritional Information (per serving): Calories: 270 (without walnuts), Protein: 6g, Fat: 3.5g, (Saturated: 0.5g, if using water), Carbohydrates: 55g, Fiber: 8g, Sugar: 15g, (natural and added), Sodium: 60mg

Chef's Tips:
1. For a smoother feel, select almond milk rather than water as it gives a delicate nutty taste which goes well with cinnamon and apples.
2. Add in a spoonful of almond butter or a scoop of your preferred protein powder after cooking for an extra protein kick.
3. If you like more fiber and texture in your oatmeal, keep the apple skin on.
4. To find what is most ideal for your taste buds, try out various apple varieties that have different levels of sweetness or tartness.

ABOUT THIS RECIPE

These pancakes are a fun variation on a classic breakfast. By using blueberries and almonds, they include the anti-inflammatory properties of these two ingredients. Full of antioxidants and good fats, not only are they healthy but also very filling. Whether you have them for a nice slow weekend morning or an elaborate brunch, these pancakes are perfect!

Servings: 4
Preparation: 10 minutes
Cook time: 15 Minutes
Recipe Type: Breakfast

BLUEBERRY AND ALMOND PANCAKES – BREAKFAST

Ingredients:

- 1 cup whole wheat or almond flour
- 1 tablespoon ground flaxseed
- 1 teaspoon baking powder
- 1/4 teaspoon salt
- 1 egg, beaten
- 1 cup almond milk
- 2 tablespoons almond butter
- 1 tablespoon honey or maple syrup
- 1/2 teaspoon vanilla extract
- 1 cup fresh blueberries
- **Optional:** extra blueberries and sliced almonds for topping

Instructions:

Mix Dry Ingredients:

- In a large bowl, combine the flour, ground flaxseed, baking powder, and salt.

Combine Wet Ingredients:

- In another bowl, whisk together the beaten egg, almond milk, almond butter, honey, and vanilla extract until smooth.

Make the Batter:

- Pour the wet ingredients into the dry ingredients and stir until just combined. Be careful not to overmix. Gently fold in the blueberries.

Cook the Pancakes:

- Heat a non-stick skillet or griddle over medium heat and lightly grease it with a little oil or butter.
- Pour 1/4 cup of batter for each pancake onto the skillet. Cook for 2-3 minutes or until bubbles form on the surface and the edges start to look set.
- Flip the pancakes and cook for an additional 2-3 minutes or until golden brown and cooked through.

Serve:

- Serve the pancakes hot with additional blueberries and sliced almonds on top, along with a drizzle of honey or maple syrup if desired.

Nutritional Information (per serving): Calories: 280, Protein: 8g, Fat: 15g (Saturated: 2g), Carbohydrates: 32g, Fiber: 5g, Sugar: 10g, Sodium: 200mg

Chef's Tips:

1. To make gluten-free pancakes, substitute whole wheat flour with gluten-free oat flour or a gluten-free all-purpose flour blend. **2.** Save morning time by preparing the batter overnight and refrigerating it. **3.** Improving taste and increasing anti-inflammatory properties can be done by including a touch of cinnamon in the mixture.

ABOUT THIS RECIPE

For a fun morning bite, try this Avocado and Egg Breakfast Pizza that brings together the smoothness of avocado and the taste of eggs, all on top of a crunchy crust. This recipe is great for a slow weekend breakfast or even a fancy brunch because it not only tastes good but also contains healthy fats like omega-3s found in eggs and mono-saturated from avocados which are anti-inflammatory too!

Servings: 2
Preparation: 10 minutes
Cook time: 15 Minutes
Recipe Type: Breakfast

AVOCADO AND EGG BREAKFAST PIZZA – BREAKFAST

Ingredients:
- 2 whole grain naan or pita bread
- 1 ripe avocado
- 2 eggs
- 1/2 cup cherry tomatoes, halved
- 1/4 red onion, thinly sliced
- 1/4 cup feta cheese, crumbled
- 1 tablespoon olive oil
- Salt and pepper to taste
- Fresh arugula for topping
- Optional: red pepper flakes or hot sauce for extra spice

Instructions:

Preheat the Oven:
- Preheat your oven to 400°F (200°C).

Prepare the Base:
- Brush each naan or pita bread lightly with olive oil. Place on a baking sheet.

Mash the Avocado:
- In a bowl, mash the avocado with a fork until creamy. Season with salt and pepper.
- Spread the mashed avocado evenly over the surface of each naan or pita bread.

Add Toppings:
- Arrange sliced red onion and cherry tomatoes over the mashed avocado.
- Carefully crack an egg into the center of each pizza.

Bake:
- Bake in the preheated oven for 10-15 minutes, or until the egg whites are set but yolks are still slightly runny (or to your preference).

Final Touches:
- Sprinkle crumbled feta cheese over each pizza.
- Add fresh arugula and optional red pepper flakes or a drizzle of hot sauce before serving.

Nutritional Information (per serving): Calories: 450, Protein: 14g, Fat: 27g, (Saturated: 6g), Carbohydrates: 36g, Fiber: 6g, Sugar: 4g, Sodium: 320mg

Chef's Tips:
1. Precook naan or pita bread for 5 minutes to make the crust crisper before putting on toppings.
2. To include more flavor and protein, you can spread hummus under the avocado.
3. Take note of how cooked the egg is because you might want to change it depending on if you like your yolk runny or hard.

ABOUT THIS RECIPE

Chia Pudding with Fresh Berries is a tasty and healthy recipe that marries the strong anti-inflammatory perks of chia seeds with fresh berries' rich antioxidants. This meal can be taken for breakfast or as a light snack; hence it supplies ample fiber, Omega-3 fats and key minerals. Preparing it is a breeze, and one can make some in advance to save on time during meals.

Servings: 2
Preparation: 10 minutes
Cook time: 0 mint (+ at least 4hrs of refrigeration)
Recipe Type: SNACK

CHIA PUDDING WITH FRESH BERRIES – BREAKFAST

Ingredients:
- ¼ cup chia seeds
- 1 cup unsweetened almond milk (or any plant-based milk of your choice)
- 1 tablespoon honey or maple syrup (optional, for sweetness)
- ½ teaspoon vanilla extract
- 1 cup mixed fresh berries (such as blueberries, strawberries, and raspberries)
- **Optional toppings:** a sprinkle of cinnamon, a few mint leaves, or a dollop of almond butter

Instructions:

Mix the Chia Base:
- In a mixing bowl, combine the chia seeds, almond milk, honey (if using), and vanilla extract. Stir well until the mixture is thoroughly combined.

Let It Set:
- Cover the bowl with a lid or plastic wrap and refrigerate for at least 4 hours, ideally overnight, until the chia seeds have absorbed the liquid and the mixture has a pudding-like consistency.

Prepare the Berries:
- Wash the fresh berries and slice any larger ones into bite-sized pieces.

Assemble the Pudding:
- Stir the chia pudding after it has set to ensure a uniform texture. Divide the pudding into serving bowls or glasses.
- Top with the fresh berries and any additional toppings you like.

Nutritional Information (per serving): Calories: 215, Protein: 5g, Fat: 9g, (Saturated: 0.5 g, Omega-3: 7 g), Carbohydrates: 29g, Fiber: 10g, Sugar: 12g (varies with the use of honey and types of berries), Sodium: 45 mg

Chef's Tips:
1. To attain the finest taste and consistency, it is advisable to leave the chia pudding overnight. This gives enough time for the seeds to absorb all the moisture and become soft.
2. Make your chia pudding unique by trying out various kinds of milk like coconut milk that gives a tropical flavor or oat milk which makes it creamier.
3. If you are serving this meal to visitors or during an occasion, put layers of berries within the chia puddings in transparent cups so that it can have an attractive look.

LUNCH

ABOUT THIS RECIPE

A delicious and nutritious recipe, the Chia Pudding with Fresh Berries combines chia seeds' powerful anti-inflammatory qualities with fresh berries' antioxidant-rich properties. It can be used for breakfast or as a light meal, providing lots of fibre, omega-3 fats and vital minerals. You can make it in advance which makes this dish convenient for quick meals.

Servings: 2
Preparation: 15 minutes
Cook time: 0 mint (assuming chicken is pre-cooked)
Recipe Type: SALAD

AVOCADO CHICKEN SALAD – LUNCH

Ingredients:

- 1 large cooked chicken breast, diced
- 1 ripe avocado, peeled and mashed
- ¼ cup red onion, finely chopped
- ½ celery stalk, diced
- Juice of 1 lime
- Salt and pepper to taste
- **Optional:** 1 tablespoon chopped cilantro or parsley for extra flavor

Instructions:

Prepare Ingredients:

- In a medium bowl, combine the diced chicken, mashed avocado, chopped red onion, and diced celery.
- Add lime juice to the mixture. This not only adds flavor but also helps keep the avocado from browning.

Mix the Salad:

- In a medium bowl, combine the diced chicken, mashed avocado, chopped red onion, and diced celery.
- Add lime juice to the mixture. This not only adds flavor but also helps keep the avocado from browning.

Chill and Serve:

- In a medium bowl, combine the diced chicken, mashed avocado, chopped red onion, and diced celery.
- Add lime juice to the mixture. This not only adds flavor but also helps keep the avocado from browning.

Nutritional Information (per serving): Calories: 290, Protein: 25g, Fat: 17g, (Saturated: 3g, Monounsaturated: 10g), Carbohydrates: 8g, Fiber: 5g, Sugar: 2g, Sodium: 200mg

Chef's Tips:

1. Combine the chicken, avocado, onion and celery in a medium bowl.
2. Mix lime juice with the ingredients; this prevents avocado from turning brown while adding flavor to them.

ABOUT THIS RECIPE

This wholesome lentil soup with kale is a nutritious dish which mixes the strong tastes of earthly lentils with the healthful, anti-inflammatory properties of kale. It is great for your body's defense system, taking care of your heart and fighting against inflammation. This soup is not only yummy but also very good for people on an anti-inflammatory diet because it can be eaten as a light lunch or served hot as dinner during cold weather.

Servings: 4
Preparation: 10 minutes
Cook time: 45 minutes
Recipe Type: SOUP

LENTIL SOUP WITH KALE – LUNCH

Ingredients:

- 1 cup dried green lentils, rinsed and drained
- 1 large onion, chopped
- 2 carrots, peeled and diced
- 2 stalks celery, diced
- 3 cloves garlic, minced
- 4 cups vegetable broth
- 2 cups water
- 1 teaspoon ground turmeric
- 1 teaspoon ground cumin
- ½ teaspoon black pepper
- ½ teaspoon salt, or to taste
- 2 cups kale, stems removed and leaves chopped
- 1 tablespoon olive oil
- **Optional:** lemon wedges and fresh chopped parsley for garnish

Instructions:

Sauté Vegetables:

- In a large pot, heat the olive oil over medium heat. Add the onion, carrots, and celery, and sauté for about 5 minutes until the vegetables begin to soften.
- Add the garlic and sauté for another minute until fragrant.

Cook the Lentils:

- Stir in the lentils, vegetable broth, water, turmeric, cumin, black pepper, and salt. Bring the mixture to a boil.
- Reduce the heat to low, cover, and simmer for about 35 minutes, or until the lentils are tender.

Add the Kale:

- Stir in the chopped kale and continue to simmer for another 5-10 minutes, until the kale is wilted and tender.

Serve:

- Adjust the seasoning if necessary. Serve the soup hot, garnished with lemon wedges and chopped parsley if desired.

Nutritional Information (per serving): Calories: 240, Protein: 14g, Fat: 4g, (Saturated: 0.5g), Carbohydrates: 38g, Fiber: 16g, Sugar: 5g, Sodium: 300mg

Chef's Tips:

1. For a taste that is more rich in flavor, you could sauté vegetables using olive oil and a small amount of butter.
2. To make the flavor better and improve its taste, add few drops of lemon before serving it.
3. This soup can be frozen; therefore, cook two batches and keep some for quick healthy meals on busy days.

ABOUT THIS RECIPE

Quinoa Stuffed Peppers is an excellent choice for an anti-inflammatory diet because it is a colorful and healthy meal made from quinoa and mixed vegetables that are rich in fiber. Not only do these peppers look good but they also contain a lot of nutrition which can help fight against inflammation like antioxidants found in bell pepper and proteins sourced from quinoa. This dish can be used as either a heavy lunch or a fulfilling dinner.

Servings: 4
Preparation: 20 minutes
Cook time: 30 minutes
Recipe Type: MAIN DISH

QUINOA STUFFED PEPPERS – LUNCH

Ingredients:
- 4 large bell peppers, tops cut away and seeds removed
- 1 cup quinoa, rinsed
- 2 cups vegetable broth
- 1 medium onion, chopped
- 2 cloves garlic, minced
- 1 zucchini, diced
- 1 cup diced tomatoes
- ½ cup corn kernels (fresh or frozen)
- 1 teaspoon olive oil
- ½ teaspoon ground cumin
- ½ teaspoon paprika
- Salt and pepper, to taste
- **Optional:** ¼ cup chopped fresh cilantro or parsley for garnish

Instructions:

Cook Quinoa:
- In a medium saucepan, combine quinoa and vegetable broth. Bring to a boil, then cover and reduce to a simmer for 15 minutes, or until all the liquid is absorbed. Set aside.

Prepare the Vegetable Filling:
- Heat olive oil in a skillet over medium heat. Add onion and garlic, sautéing until onions are translucent.
- Add zucchini and cook for an additional 5 minutes until slightly soft.
- Stir in the cooked quinoa, diced tomatoes, corn, cumin, paprika, salt, and pepper. Cook for another 5 minutes, stirring occasionally.

Stuff the Peppers:
- Preheat oven to 375°F (190°C).
- Spoon the quinoa and vegetable mixture into each hollowed-out pepper, packing it tightly.

Bake:
- Place stuffed peppers upright in a baking dish. Cover with foil and bake for 25-30 minutes, until the peppers are tender.

Serve:
- Garnish with chopped cilantro or parsley if desired.

Nutritional Information (per serving): Calories: 250, Protein: 8g, Fat: 4g, (Saturated: 0.5g), Carbohydrates: 45g, Fiber: 8g, Sugar: 9g, Sodium: 300mg

Chef's Tips:
1. For a protein boost, consider adding a can of drained and rinsed black beans to the quinoa mixture before stuffing the peppers. **2.** If you like a crispy top, sprinkle a small amount of grated parmesan or vegan cheese alternative over each pepper before baking. **3.** Quinoa stuffed peppers can be made in advance and refrigerated for a quick reheat on busy days, making them perfect for meal prep.

ABOUT THIS RECIPE

The Turkey and Spinach Wrap is a delicious and healthy choice for lunch or a fast dinner. It contains low-fat turkey, new spinach, and a whole grain wrap that are full of anti-inflammatory substances. It helps the body to recover in general and fights sicknesses because it has lean protein, fiber, and antioxidants which are excellent against inflammation.

Servings: 2
Preparation: 10 minutes
Cook time: 0 minutes
Recipe Type: Lunch/Dinner

TURKEY AND SPINACH WRAP – LUNCH

Ingredients:

- 2 whole-grain wraps
- 6 ounces of sliced turkey breast (preferably organic or low-sodium)
- 1 cup fresh spinach leaves, washed and dried
- ½ avocado, sliced
- ¼ cup shredded carrots
- 2 tablespoons hummus
- Salt and pepper, to taste
- **Optional:** 1 tablespoon cranberries or sliced almonds for added texture and flavor

Instructions:

Prepare the Ingredients:

- Lay out the whole-grain wraps on a clean surface.
- Spread 1 tablespoon of hummus on each wrap.

Assemble the Wraps:

- Distribute the sliced turkey evenly across the wraps.
- Top with fresh spinach leaves and shredded carrots.
- Add avocado slices evenly on top of the greens.
- If using, sprinkle cranberries or sliced almonds over the ingredients.
- Season with salt and pepper to taste.

Wrap It Up:

- Carefully fold the sides of the wrap inward and then roll the wrap tightly from bottom to top to enclose all the fillings.
- Cut the wraps in half diagonally to serve.

Nutritional Information (per serving): Calories: 350 Protein: 25g, Fat: 15g, (Saturated: 2.5g), Carbohydrates: 27g, Fiber: 6g, Sugar: 4g, Sodium: 620mg

Chef's Tips:

1. For maximum flavor, choose preservative-free turkey breast of high quality. Smoked turkey is also a good choice.
2. Warm the wrap slightly so that it rolls easily without tearing.
3. This wrap is very adaptable – feel free to include other vegetables such as sliced bell peppers or cucumber for added crunch and nutrition.
4. If you're making this wrap ahead of time, wrap it tightly in parchment paper or aluminum foil to keep it fresh and prevent it from getting soggy.

ABOUT THIS RECIPE

The Mediterranean Chickpea Salad is a nutritious and colorful dish that represents the Mediterranean diet and has great anti-inflammatory properties. It contains lots of fiber, proteins and good fats from chickpeas, olives and olive oil; thus making it more than just tasty lunch or side salad but also a strong weapon against inflammation.

Servings: 4
Preparation: 15 minutes
Cook time: 0 minutes
Recipe Type: SALAD

MEDITERRANEAN CHICKPEA SALAD – LUNCH

Ingredients:

- 2 cups cooked chickpeas (or one 15-ounce can, drained and rinsed)
- 1 cucumber, diced
- 1 bell pepper, any color, diced
- 1 small red onion, finely chopped
- 1 cup cherry tomatoes, halved
- 1/3 cup pitted Kalamata olives, halved
- ¼ cup feta cheese, crumbled (optional)
- ¼ cup fresh parsley, chopped
- 3 tablespoons extra virgin olive oil
- 2 tablespoons lemon juice
- 1 teaspoon dried oregano
- Salt and pepper, to taste

Instructions:

Combine Salad Ingredients:

- In a large mixing bowl, combine the chickpeas, cucumber, bell pepper, red onion, cherry tomatoes, olives, and parsley.

Prepare the Dressing:

- In a small bowl or jar, whisk together the olive oil, lemon juice, oregano, salt, and pepper until well blended.

Toss and Chill:

- Pour the dressing over the salad and toss to coat all the ingredients evenly.
- Sprinkle crumbled feta cheese over the top.
- Refrigerate the salad for at least 30 minutes before serving to allow the flavors to meld.

Nutritional Information (per serving): Calories: 260, Protein: 7g, Fat: 15g, (Saturated: 3g), Carbohydrates: 27g, Fiber: 6g, Sugar: 5g, Sodium: 320mg

Chef's Tips:

1. To get the best taste, refrigerate the salad for a few hours or overnight so that chickpeas can suck up the dressing and flavors become more intense.
2. Being flexible is one of the advantages of this salad; you may include other Mediterranean items such as artichokes, roasted red peppers or even sprinkle some sumac on top to make it tangier.
3. You can serve it alone or with grilled fish or chicken to add protein..

ABOUT THIS RECIPE

This dish is full of nutrients and colors. It can be eaten at any time. Beets have many antioxidants and anti-inflammatory compounds, which are widely known. Goat cheese adds protein and a creamy texture that is pleasant. In addition to the fact that it tastes good on its own, this salad also has tangy vinaigrette dressing that helps fight inflammation and improve well-being in general

Servings: 2
Preparation: 10 minutes
Cook time: 45 minutes
Recipe Type: SALAD

ROASTED BEET AND GOAT CHEESE SALAD – LUNCH

Ingredients:

- 3 medium beets, peeled and diced
- 2 tablespoons olive oil
- Salt and pepper, to taste
- 4 cups mixed salad greens
- ½ cup crumbled goat cheese
- ¼ cup walnuts, toasted and chopped

For the vinaigrette:

- 3 tablespoons balsamic vinegar
- 1 tablespoon Dijon mustard
- 1 tablespoon honey
- ¼ cup olive oil
- Salt and pepper, to taste

Instructions:

Roast the Beets:

- Preheat your oven to 400°F (200°C).
- Toss the diced beets with 2 tablespoons of olive oil, salt, and pepper. Spread them on a baking sheet.
- Roast in the preheated oven for about 45 minutes, or until tender and caramelized, stirring halfway through for even cooking.

Prepare the Vinaigrette:

- In a small bowl, whisk together balsamic vinegar, Dijon mustard, honey, and ¼ cup olive oil until emulsified. Season with salt and pepper to taste.

Assemble the Salad:

- In a large salad bowl, combine the mixed greens, roasted beets, crumbled goat cheese, and toasted walnuts.
- Drizzle with the prepared vinaigrette and toss gently to coat all the ingredients evenly.

Nutritional Information (per serving): Calories: 410, Protein: 10g, Fat: 32g, (Saturated: 7g), Carbohydrates: 24g, Fiber: 6g, Sugar: 17g, Sodium: 300mg

Chef's Tips:

1. By roasting beets, their sweetness is intensified so that they can provide an ideal contrast against the sourness of goat cheese. In order to achieve the best taste, it is advised that you roast them until they start to caramelize.
2. Beets may be roasted beforehand and refrigerated in order to save time on the day of the meal. They make for a great salad addition served either cold or at room temperature.
3. If you want more texture and flavor, try adding some fresh herbs like thyme or parsley.

ABOUT THIS RECIPE

The hummus tartine with vegetables is a good open sandwich which combines the crunchy mixed vegetables with the smooth creamy taste of hummus. It can be eaten as a healthy snack or even light lunch that is rich in fiber, vitamins and antioxidants that fight inflammation and enhance general health.

Servings: 2
Preparation: 10 minutes
Cook time: 0 minutes
Recipe Type: SNACK

VEGETABLE AND HUMMUS TARTINE – LUNCH

Ingredients:

- 2 slices of whole-grain bread
- ½ cup hummus (homemade or store-bought)
- ¼ cucumber, thinly sliced
- 1 small carrot, julienned or grated
- ¼ red bell pepper, thinly sliced
- ¼ avocado, sliced
- 1 radish, thinly sliced
- 1 tablespoon olive oil
- 1 tablespoon lemon juice
- Salt and pepper, to taste
- **Optional:** sprouts or microgreens for garnish

Instructions:

Prepare the Vegetables:

- Wash and slice the cucumber, bell pepper, radish, and avocado. Grate or julienne the carrot.

Toast the Bread:

- Lightly toast the whole-grain bread slices until golden and crisp.

Assemble the Tartine:

- Spread a generous layer of hummus on each slice of toasted bread.
- Arrange the cucumber, carrot, bell pepper, avocado, and radish slices neatly over the hummus.
- Drizzle with olive oil and lemon juice, then season with salt and pepper.

Garnish and Serve:

- Add sprouts or microgreens, if using, for an extra touch of flavor and nutrition.
- Serve immediately to enjoy the crispness of the vegetables and bread.

Nutritional Information (per serving): Calories: 265, Protein: 8g, Fat: 14g, (Saturated: 2g), Carbohydrates: 29g Fiber: 7g, Sodium: 390mg

Chef's Tips:

1. To make the recipe gluten free, the base can be made with gluten free bread or large lettuce leaves.
2. For more taste, add some za'atar mix or chili flakes on top of the tartine.
3. It is recommended to prepare vegetables ahead and refrigerate them for busy days.

DINNER

ABOUT THIS RECIPE

This Turmeric Roasted Chicken with Cauliflower recipe is a flavorful and healthful dish that makes use of turmeric, a powerful anti-inflammatory spice. Alongside nutrient-rich cauliflower, this meal is designed to boost your immune system and fight inflammation, all while delivering a delicious, satisfying dinner.

Servings: 4
Preparation: 15 minutes
Cook time: 40 minutes
Recipe Type: DINNER

TURMERIC ROASTED CHICKEN WITH CAULIFLOWER – DINNER

Ingredients:

- 4 chicken thighs (bone-in, skin-on)
- 1 large head of cauliflower, cut into florets
- 2 tablespoons olive oil
- 1 teaspoon turmeric
- ½ teaspoon garlic powder
- ½ teaspoon paprika
- Salt and black pepper, to taste
- Fresh parsley, chopped (for garnish)

Instructions:

Preheat the Oven and Prepare Pans:

- Preheat your oven to 400°F (200°C). Line a baking sheet with parchment paper or a silicone mat for easy cleanup.

Season the Chicken and Cauliflower:

- In a large bowl, combine olive oil, turmeric, garlic powder, paprika, salt, and pepper. Mix well to create a marinade.
- Add the chicken thighs and cauliflower florets to the bowl. Toss well to ensure they are thoroughly coated with the marinade.

Roast:

- Arrange the chicken and cauliflower in a single layer on the prepared baking sheet.
- Roast in the preheated oven for about 40 minutes, or until the chicken is golden and reaches an internal temperature of 165°F (74°C) and the cauliflower is tender and caramelized.

Serve:

- Remove from oven and let rest for a few minutes.
- Garnish with chopped parsley before serving.

Nutritional Information (per serving): Calories: 350, Protein: 25g, Fat: 26g, (Saturated: 6g), Carbohydrates: 8g, Fiber: 3g, Sodium: 320mg

Chef's Tips:

1. For an even more flavorful dish, marinate the chicken and cauliflower in the turmeric mixture for at least an hour or overnight in the refrigerator before roasting.
2. If you prefer a bit of a spicy kick, add a pinch of cayenne pepper to the marinade.
3. Serve this dish with a side of whole grain rice or quinoa to make a complete meal that's both satisfying and anti-inflammatory.

ABOUT THIS RECIPE

This quick and tasty meal is good for any day of the week. Grilled Shrimp with Garlic Broccoli combines omega-3 fatty acids found in shrimp (known as a healthy fat) with broccoli an anti-inflammatory powerhouse loaded with antioxidants. It's perfect if you want something light but still flavorful while taking care of yourself at the same time!

Servings: 2
Preparation: 10 minutes
Cook time: 10 minutes
Recipe Type: Main Course

GRILLED SHRIMP WITH GARLIC BROCCOLI – DINNER

Ingredients:

- 12 large shrimp, peeled and deveined
- 2 cups broccoli florets
- 3 tablespoons olive oil
- 2 cloves garlic, minced
- 1 lemon, zest and juice
- Salt and pepper, to taste
- **Optional:** red pepper flakes for added heat

Instructions:

Preheat the Grill:
- Preheat your grill to medium-high heat.

Prepare the Shrimp:
- In a bowl, toss the shrimp with 1 tablespoon of olive oil, half of the minced garlic, lemon zest, and a pinch of salt and pepper.
- If desired, add red pepper flakes for a spicy kick.

Grill the Shrimp:
- Thread the shrimp onto skewers and place on the grill.
- Grill for about 2-3 minutes per side or until the shrimp are opaque and slightly charred.

Prepare the Broccoli:
- While the shrimp are grilling, heat the remaining olive oil in a large skillet over medium heat.
- Add the remaining garlic and sauté until fragrant, about 1 minute.
- Add the broccoli florets and toss to coat in the garlic oil. Season with salt and pepper.
- Sauté the broccoli until it is bright green and tender-crisp, about 5-6 minutes.
- Finish by adding a squeeze of fresh lemon juice for extra flavor.

Serve:
- Arrange the grilled shrimp and garlic broccoli on plates.
- Serve with a wedge of lemon on the side for added zest.

Nutritional Information (per serving): Calories: 300, Protein: 25g, Fat: 20g (Saturated: 3g), Carbohydrates: 8g Fiber: 3g, Sugar: 2g, Sodium: 480mg

Chef's Tips:
1. For the best flavor, let the shrimp marinate in the garlic and olive oil mixture for about 10-15 minutes before grilling.
3. Use fresh lemon juice not only for marinating the shrimp but also to enhance the taste of the broccoli once it's cooked.
4. For a complete meal, serve this dish over a bed of quinoa or alongside a fresh salad.

ABOUT THIS RECIPE

Lemon and Dill Trout Baked is an easy-to-make dish that combines the delicious taste of fresh trout with the tangy, fragrant lemon and dill. Not only this recipe tasty but also full of omega-3 fatty acids which have anti-inflammatory effects in our bodies. This meal is good for dinner because it is light in calories and very nutritious too!

Servings: 2
Preparation: 10 minutes
Cook time: 15 minutes
Recipe Type: DINNER

BAKED TROUT WITH LEMON AND DILL – DINNER

Ingredients:

- 2 trout fillets (about 6 ounces each)
- 2 tablespoons olive oil
- 1 lemon, thinly sliced
- 2 tablespoons fresh dill, chopped
- Salt and freshly ground black pepper, to taste

Instructions:

Preheat the Oven:
- Preheat your oven to 375°F (190°C).

Prepare the Trout:
- Rinse the trout fillets under cold water and pat dry with paper towels.
- Place each fillet on a piece of aluminum foil large enough to fold over and seal.

Season the Fish:
- Drizzle each fillet with olive oil and season generously with salt and pepper.
- Place lemon slices on top of the fillets and sprinkle with chopped dill.

Bake the Trout:
- Fold the foil over the trout, sealing the edges to create a packet that will keep the steam in while the fish bakes.
- Place the foil packets on a baking sheet and bake in the preheated oven for 15 minutes, or until the trout is opaque and flakes easily with a fork.

Serve:
- Carefully open the foil packets (watch for steam), and transfer the fillets to plates.
- Serve immediately, garnished with additional dill and lemon slices if desired.

Nutritional Information (per serving): Calories: 295, Protein: 25g, Fat: 20g (Saturated: 3g, Omega-3: ~1g) Carbohydrates: 2g, Fiber: 0.5g, Sodium: 58mg

Chef's Tips:
1. To achieve the best taste and texture, make it certain that your trout is fresh; a fresh fish does not smell strongly of fish. **2.** Depending on how thickly your fillets are cut, you may have to adjust the cooking time by a few minutes. **3.** If you want even more flavor, pour some white wine into the foil before putting it in the oven so that trout can be baked within this packet.

ABOUT THIS RECIPE

This dish is full of life and flavor. It contains lean proteins, colorful vegetables, and anti-inflammatory spices as well. Additionally, it is easy to make and has a lot of vitamins which can help lower swelling in the body so that you don't have to sacrifice taste when choosing healthier options for dinner.

Servings: 2
Preparation: 15 minutes
Cook time: 10 minutes
Recipe Type: DINNER

BEEF STIR-FRY WITH BELL PEPPERS AND BROCCOLI – DINNER

Ingredients:

- 8 oz lean beef, thinly sliced (such as flank steak or sirloin)
- 1 red bell pepper, thinly sliced
- 1 green bell pepper, thinly sliced
- 1 cup broccoli florets
- 2 cloves garlic, minced
- 1 tablespoon ginger, grated
- 2 tablespoons olive oil
- 2 tablespoons low-sodium soy sauce
- 1 tablespoon oyster sauce (optional)
- 1 teaspoon sesame oil
- Salt and black pepper, to taste
- **Optional garnish:** sesame seeds, green onions

Instructions:

Prepare the Ingredients:

Wash and cut the bell peppers and broccoli into bite-sized pieces. Thinly slice the beef and set aside.

Marinate the Beef:

In a bowl, mix the soy sauce, oyster sauce (if using), and sesame oil. Add the beef slices and toss to coat. Let marinate for at least 10 minutes.

Stir-Fry the Vegetables:

Heat 1 tablespoon of olive oil in a large skillet or wok over medium-high heat.

Add the garlic and ginger and sauté for about 30 seconds until fragrant.

Add the broccoli and bell peppers, stir-frying for about 3-4 minutes until they are just tender but still crisp.

Cook the Beef:

Push the vegetables to the side of the skillet, add the remaining tablespoon of olive oil, and place the marinated beef in the center. Stir-fry for about 2-3 minutes until the beef is cooked through and slightly browned.

Combine and Serve:

Mix the vegetables and beef together in the skillet. Season with salt and pepper to taste.

Serve hot, garnished with sesame seeds and chopped green onions if desired.

Nutritional Information (per serving): Calories: 345, Protein: 26g, Fat: 22g, (Saturated: 4g), Carbohydrates: 12g, Fiber: 3g, Sugar: 5g, Sodium: 630mg (varies depending on the use of soy sauce and oyster sauce)

Chef's Tips: 1. For the best texture and ease of cooking, freeze the beef slightly before slicing. This makes it easier to cut thin, even slices. 2. Always preheat the wok or skillet to ensure that the vegetables and meat sauté quickly, retaining their texture and flavors. 3. Adjust the soy sauce and sesame oil according to your taste and sodium preferences. For a gluten-free option, use tamari instead of soy sauce.

ABOUT THIS RECIPE

A yummy, nutrient packed meal that brings together the omega-3 fatty acids of salmon and the fiber and vitamins of asparagus is Herb-Crusted Salmon with Asparagus. It doesn't only taste great; it has anti-inflammatory properties too! Therefore, this recipe is perfect for a dinner which cares for health yet satisfies taste buds.

Servings: 4
Preparation: 15 minutes
Cook time: 20 minutes
Recipe Type: DINNER

HERB-CRUSTED SALMON WITH ASPARAGUS – DINNER

Ingredients:
- 2 salmon fillets (6 oz each)
- 1 bunch of asparagus, ends trimmed
- 2 tablespoons olive oil
- 1 lemon (half juiced, half sliced)
- 2 tablespoons fresh parsley, finely chopped
- 2 tablespoons fresh dill, finely chopped
- 1 clove garlic, minced
- ¼ cup whole wheat breadcrumbs (or gluten-free alternative)
- Salt and pepper, to taste

Instructions:

Preheat the Oven:
- Preheat your oven to 400°F (200°C).

Prepare the Herb Crust:
- In a small bowl, mix together the breadcrumbs, minced garlic, chopped parsley, dill, half of the lemon juice, and 1 tablespoon olive oil. Season with salt and pepper.

Prepare the Asparagus:
- Toss the asparagus spears with the remaining olive oil and a pinch of salt and pepper. Lay them in a single layer on one side of a baking sheet.

Assemble the Salmon:
- Place the salmon fillets on the other side of the baking sheet.
- Spoon the herb-breadcrumb mixture generously over each salmon fillet, pressing slightly to adhere.

Bake:
- Place the baking sheet in the oven and bake for about 15-20 minutes, or until the salmon is opaque and flakes easily with a fork and the asparagus is tender.

Serve:
- Serve the herb-crusted salmon and asparagus hot, garnished with lemon slices and a drizzle of the remaining lemon juice.

Nutritional Information (per serving): Calories: 425, Protein: 35g, Fat: 25g, (Saturated: 4g, Omega-3:~2g) Carbohydrates: 15g, Fiber: 4g, Sugar: 3g, Sodium: 300mg

Chef's Tips:
1. To make the herb crust stick better, pat dry the salmon fillets using a paper towel.
2. You can use gluten-free bread crumbs or a combination of almond meal and finely chopped nuts in place of breadcrumbs to achieve a gluten-free alternative.
3. If you want a crisper topping, broil the salmon for the last 2-3 minutes.

ABOUT THIS RECIPE

The dish has vibrant colors and succulent lamb chops combined with refreshing mint pesto served alongside some filling roasted vegetables. This is ideal for people who would like to have a dinner that is rich in proteins, flavorsome as well as anti-inflammatory due to the presence of fresh herbs and antioxidant packed vegetables in it.

Servings: 2
Preparation: 15 minutes
Cook time: 25 minutes
Recipe Type: DINNER

LAMB CHOPS WITH MINT PESTO AND ROASTED VEGGIES – DINNER

Ingredients:
- 4 lamb chops
- 2 tablespoons olive oil
- Salt and pepper, to taste
- 1 small zucchini, sliced
- 1 red bell pepper, cut into strips
- 1 medium sweet potato, peeled and cubed
- 1 small red onion, cut into wedges

For the Mint Pesto:
- 1 cup fresh mint leaves
- 1/2 cup fresh parsley leaves
- 1/4 cup walnuts, toasted
- 2 cloves garlic, minced
- 1/3 cup olive oil
- 2 tablespoons lemon juice
- Salt and pepper, to taste

Instructions:

Prepare the Vegetables:
- Preheat the oven to 400°F (200°C).
- Toss the zucchini, bell pepper, sweet potato, and red onion with olive oil, salt, and pepper.
- Spread the vegetables on a baking sheet and roast for about 20-25 minutes, until tender and caramelized.

Make the Mint Pesto:
- In a food processor, combine mint leaves, parsley, toasted walnuts, and garlic.
- Pulse while gradually adding olive oil and lemon juice until the mixture reaches a coarse but spreadable consistency.
- Season with salt and pepper to taste.

Cook the Lamb Chops:
- Season the lamb chops with salt and pepper.
- Heat olive oil in a skillet over medium-high heat.
- Add the lamb chops and cook for about 3-4 minutes per side for medium-rare, or until they reach the desired doneness.

Serve:
- Plate the roasted vegetables alongside the cooked lamb chops.
- Spoon the mint pesto over the lamb chops just before serving.

Nutritional Information (per serving): Calories: 650, Protein: 38g, Fat: 48g, (Saturated: 10g), Carbohydrates: 25g, Fiber: 5g, Sodium: 220mg

Chef's Tips:
1. To make a pesto without nuts, use sunflower or pumpkin seeds instead of walnuts.
2. For the lamb chops to be juicy and flavorful, let them rest for a few minutes after cooking.
3. Prepare the mint pesto ahead of time and refrigerate it for up to one week or freeze it for later use.

ABOUT THIS RECIPE

This Pesto Pasta with Pine Nuts and Sun-Dried Tomatoes is a flavorful, lively dish which combines the pungent richness of pesto with the sweet tang of sun-dried tomatoes and the nutty bite of pine nuts. It's a healthy but filling dinner that packs in plenty of anti-inflammatory foods like basil, garlic and olive oil; these are all commonly found in Mediterranean diets that support heart health and lower inflammation levels.

Servings: 4
Preparation: 15 minutes
Cook time: 04 minutes
Recipe Type: DINNER

PESTO PASTA WITH SUN-DRIED TOMATOES AND PINE NUTS – DINNER

Ingredients:
- 12 oz whole grain or gluten-free pasta
- ½ cup homemade or store-bought pesto
- ¼ cup sun-dried tomatoes, chopped
- ¼ cup pine nuts, toasted
- 2 cloves garlic, minced
- 2 tbsp extra virgin olive oil
- Salt and freshly ground black pepper, to taste
- Optional: Fresh basil leaves for garnish
- **Optional:** Grated Parmesan cheese or nutritional yeast for a dairy-free option

Instructions:

Cook the Pasta:
- Bring a large pot of salted water to a boil. Add pasta and cook according to package instructions until al dente. Drain and set aside, reserving 1/2 cup of the pasta water to thin the sauce if needed.

Prepare the Add-Ins:
- While the pasta cooks, heat olive oil in a small skillet over medium heat. Add garlic and sauté until fragrant, about 1 minute. Add the sun-dried tomatoes and toasted pine nuts, stir to combine, and cook for another 2 minutes. Remove from heat.

Combine Ingredients:
- In a large bowl, mix the cooked pasta with the pesto. Add the garlic, sun-dried tomatoes, and pine nuts mixture. Toss well to combine. If the pasta seems dry, add a little reserved pasta water to reach the desired consistency.

Serve:
- Season with salt and pepper to taste. Garnish with fresh basil leaves and grated Parmesan cheese or nutritional yeast if using.

Nutritional Information (per serving): Calories: 450, Protein: 14g, Fat: 22g (Saturated: 3g) Carbohydrates: 52g Fiber: 8g, Sodium: 320mg

Chef's Tips:
1. For more taste, you may add capers or black olives to the dish.
2. To increase the amount of protein in it, grill some chicken or add chickpeas.
3. Do not overcook the pasta; al dente is not only tastier but also has a lower glycemic index.

WEEK 3 MEAL PLAN

Day	Breakfast	Lunch	Dinner
Monday	Chia Coconut Yogurt Parfait	Broccoli and Almond Soup	Grilled Tuna Steaks with Olive Tapenade
Tuesday	Avocado Berry Smoothie	Roast Beef Wrap with Arugula and Horseradish	Stuffed Acorn Squash with Quinoa and Cranberries
Wednesday	Pumpkin Oatmeal	Lentil and Vegetable Stew	Rosemary Lemon Chicken with Roasted Brussels Sprouts
Thursday	Toasted Almond Butter and Banana Sandwich	Sardine Salad on Whole Grain Toast	Thai Coconut Curry with Tofu and Vegetables
Friday	Green Detox Smoothie	Tomato and White Bean Salad	Baked Salmon with Dill and Lemon Asparagus
Saturday	Egg White Omelet with Spinach and Mushrooms	Sweet Potato and Black Bean Chili	Herb Roasted Lamb with Root Vegetables
Sunday	Oatmeal with Apples and Cinnamon	Grilled Chicken Caesar Salad	Pasta Primavera with Olive Oil and Vegetables

2024 Complete Anti-Inflammatory Diet

WEEK 3 SHOPPING LIST

Produce:

- Mixed berries (strawberries, blueberries, raspberries)
- Broccoli (1 large head or equivalent)
- Lemons (4-5 for various uses)
- Avocados (several, depending on size)
- Bananas
- Pumpkin puree (canned or fresh if you prefer to make your own)
- Brussels sprouts (1 lb)
- Fresh vegetables for curry (e.g., bell peppers, carrots, zucchini)
- Asparagus (1 bunch)
- Spinach (1 large bag or bunch)
- Mushrooms (1 lb)
- Sweet potatoes (for chili)
- Root vegetables (carrots, parsnips, beets for roasting with lamb)
- Apples
- Arugula
- Tomatoes
- White beans (canned or dry if you prefer to soak and cook your own)
- Red onion
- Garlic

Protein:

- Coconut yogurt (or regular dairy yogurt if not available)
- Tuna steaks
- Roast beef slices
- Chicken breasts
- Tofu (firm or extra firm)
- Salmon fillets
- Lamb (for roasting)
- Egg whites (or whole eggs if you prefer whole egg omelets)
- Sardines

Grains & Legumes:

- Quinoa
- Whole grain wraps
- Whole grain toast or bread
- Lentils
- Pasta (whole grain or gluten-free)

Nuts & Seeds:

- Almonds (for soup and snacks)
- Chia seeds
- Walnuts (for squash stuffing)

Dairy & Alternatives:

- Horseradish sauce
- Parmesan cheese (for Caesar salad)

Pantry Staples:

- Olive oil
- Vegetable broth
- Honey
- Maple syrup
- Spices (cinnamon, rosemary, salt, pepper)
- Granola (for parfait)
- Dried cranberries
- Capers

Miscellaneous:

- Thai curry paste
- Coconut milk (for curry)

Use this shopping list for Week 3 meals. Modify it to fit your needs or lifestyle. For example, if you don't eat meat you can replace it with plant-based protein and choose gluten-free products if necessary. Have fun cooking and enjoy all the different tastes!

OPTIONAL WEEKLY PREP GUIDE

Sunday Prep:

1. **Vegetables:**

Wash and chop all vegetables needed for the week, such as broccoli, Brussels sprouts, carrots, bell peppers, zucchini, mushrooms, and root vegetables. Store them in airtight containers in the fridge.

2. **Proteins:**

- Cook chicken breasts for the Caesar salad and other dishes as needed. Store cooked chicken in the fridge.
- Marinate the lamb for Tuesday's dinner and store in the fridge to enhance the flavor.

3. **Grains and Legumes:**

- Cook a batch of quinoa for the stuffed acorn squash and other meals as required. Store in an airtight container in the fridge.
- Prepare lentils for the vegetable stew.

4. **Sauces and Dressings:**

- Prepare any dressings or sauces needed for the week, such as the olive tapenade for the tuna steaks and horseradish sauce for the wraps.

5. **Smoothie Prep:**

- Portion out fruits and vegetables for smoothies. Place them in individual bags and store them in the freezer.

Daily Preparation Tips:

Monday:

- Assemble the Chia Coconut Yogurt Parfait in the morning.
- Reheat the prepped broccoli and almond soup for lunch.
- Grill the tuna steaks and serve with pre-made olive tapenade for dinner.

Tuesday:

- Blend the Avocado Berry Smoothie for a quick breakfast.
- Assemble the roast beef wraps using prepped horseradish sauce and arugula.
- Bake the pre-stuffed acorn squash for dinner.

Wednesday:

- Cook the Pumpkin Oatmeal in the morning.
- Heat the Lentil and Vegetable Stew for lunch.
- Roast the chicken and Brussels sprouts for dinner.

Thursday:

- Make the Toasted Almond Butter and Banana Sandwich for breakfast.
- Prepare the Sardine Salad on toast for lunch.
- Cook the Thai Coconut Curry with prepped tofu and vegetables for dinner.

Friday:

- Prepare the Green Detox Smoothie in the morning.
- Toss together the Tomato and White Bean Salad for lunch.
- Bake the salmon and steam the asparagus for dinner.

Saturday:

- Cook the Egg White Omelet with prepped spinach and mushrooms for breakfast.
- Serve the Sweet Potato and Black Bean Chili for lunch.
- Roast the herb-marinated lamb with prepped root vegetables for dinner.

Sunday:

- Make Oatmeal with Apples and Cinnamon for breakfast.
- Grill chicken for the Caesar Salad at lunch.
- Prepare the Pasta Primavera for dinner using a variety of prepped vegetables.

This guideline for preparation will aid you in keeping an operational kitchen for the whole week so that you can have homemade food every day. Modify timings and tasks according to your timetable and eating habits.

WEEK 3 RECIPES

Monday:

Breakfast: Chia Coconut Yogurt Parfait

- **Ingredients:** 1 cup coconut yogurt, 2 tbsp chia seeds, ½ cup mixed berries, ¼ cup granola.
- **Instructions:** Layer the coconut yogurt and chia seeds in a glass or bowl. Top with mixed berries and granola. Serve immediately or let sit overnight in the fridge to thicken.

Lunch: Broccoli and Almond Soup

- **Ingredients:** 2 cups broccoli florets, 1 onion chopped, 2 cloves garlic minced, 4 cups vegetable broth, ½ cup toasted almonds, 1 tbsp olive oil, salt, and pepper to taste.
- **Instructions:** In a pot, sauté onion and garlic in olive oil until translucent. Add broccoli and broth, bring to a boil, then simmer until broccoli is tender. Blend the soup with toasted almonds until smooth. Season with salt and pepper.

Dinner: Grilled Tuna Steaks with Olive Tapenade

- **Ingredients:** 2 tuna steaks, ½ cup olives, 2 tbsp capers, 1 clove garlic, juice of 1 lemon, 2 tbsp olive oil, salt, and pepper.
- **Instructions:** For the tapenade, blend olives, capers, garlic, and lemon juice until coarse. Season tuna steaks with salt, pepper, and a drizzle of olive oil. Grill over medium heat until desired doneness. Serve with olive tapenade.

Tuesday:

Breakfast: Avocado Berry Smoothie

- **Ingredients:** 1 ripe avocado, 1 cup mixed berries, 1 cup spinach, 1 cup almond milk, 1 tbsp honey.
- **Instructions:** Blend all ingredients until smooth, adding more almond milk if necessary for desired consistency.

Lunch: Roast Beef Wrap with Arugula and Horseradish

- **Ingredients:** 2 whole grain wraps, 6 oz sliced roast beef, 1 cup arugula, 2 tbsp horseradish sauce.
- **Instructions:** Spread horseradish sauce on wraps, top with roast beef and arugula, roll tightly.

Dinner: Stuffed Acorn Squash with Quinoa and Cranberries

- **Ingredients:** 2 acorn squashes, halved and seeded, 1 cup cooked quinoa, ½ cup dried cranberries, ½ cup chopped walnuts, 2 tbsp maple syrup, 1 tsp cinnamon.
- **Instructions:** Bake acorn squash at 375°F until tender, about 25 minutes. Mix quinoa, cranberries, walnuts, maple syrup, and cinnamon. Fill squash halves with the mixture and bake for an additional 15 minutes.

Wednesday:

Breakfast: Pumpkin Oatmeal

- **Ingredients:** 1 cup rolled oats, 1 cup pumpkin puree, 2 cups almond milk, 1 tsp cinnamon, 1 tbsp honey.
- **Instructions:** Combine all ingredients in a pot and cook over medium heat until oats are soft and creamy.

Lunch: Lentil and Vegetable Stew

- **Ingredients:** 1 cup lentils, 1 carrot diced, 1 celery stalk diced, 1 onion diced, 4 cups vegetable broth, 2 tsp olive oil, salt, and pepper.
- **Instructions:** Sauté onion, carrot, and celery in olive oil until soft. Add lentils and broth, bring to a boil, then simmer until lentils are tender. Season with salt and pepper.

Dinner: Rosemary Lemon Chicken with Roasted Brussels Sprouts

- **Ingredients:** 4 chicken breasts, 1 lemon (juice and zest), 2 tbsp chopped rosemary, 2 cups Brussels sprouts, 2 tbsp olive oil, salt, and pepper.
- **Instructions:** Marinate chicken with lemon juice, zest, rosemary, salt, and pepper. Roast at 375°F for 25 minutes. Toss Brussels sprouts with olive oil, salt, and pepper, roast alongside chicken until crispy.

To help you combat inflammation, each of these recipe is made up of nutritious hearty flavors. The quantities and constituents can be altered to suit one's needs or taste. Have fun preparing them while staying healthy!

BREAKFAST

ABOUT THIS RECIPE

This Chia Parfait with Coconut Yogurt is a yummy, simple-to-prepare breakfast or snack that joins creamy coconut yogurt together with vitamin-packed chia seeds and tangy antioxidant berries. Not only that, but it's also great for those on anti-inflammatory diets as it supplies their bodies with omega-3 fats from the chia seeds while ensuring there are enough good bacteria in the digestive tract courtesy of probiotics found in yoghurts.

Servings: 4
Preparation: 10 minutes
Cook time: 0 minutes (plus optional refrigeration time)
Recipe Type: SNACK

CHIA COCONUT YOGURT PARFAIT – BREAKFAST

Ingredients:

- 1 cup coconut yogurt (unsweetened)
- 2 tablespoons chia seeds
- ½ cup mixed berries (such as blueberries, strawberries, and raspberries)
- ¼ cup granola (gluten-free if necessary)
- Optional: a drizzle of honey or maple syrup for added sweetness

Instructions:

Mix Chia Seeds with Yogurt:

- In a small bowl, stir the chia seeds into the coconut yogurt. Let sit for 5 minutes to allow the chia seeds to begin absorbing moisture and swell up. For a thicker consistency, let the mixture sit in the refrigerator overnight.

Layer the Ingredients:

- In a serving glass or bowl, layer half of the chia coconut yogurt mixture. Follow with a layer of half the mixed berries, then a layer of half the granola. Repeat the layers with the remaining yogurt, berries, and granola.

Garnish and Serve:

- Top with a final few berries and an optional drizzle of honey or maple syrup for extra sweetness. Serve immediately for a fresh, crunchy texture, or refrigerate for an hour for the flavors to meld together more deeply.

Nutritional Information (per serving): Calories: 350, Protein: 8g, Fat: 20g (Saturated: 8g), Carbohydrates: 35g, Fiber: 10g, Sugar: 15g (varies depending on the addition of honey/maple syrup), Sodium: 55mg

Chef's Tips:

1. To make a parfait crispy and textured, add the granola right before serving so that it stays crunchy.
2. For more variety and the most antioxidants, use various fruits in season for your parfait.
3. If you want vegan parfaits, check the granola's ingredients to make sure it doesn't have honey and swap out honey with maple syrup or another sweetener.

ABOUT THIS RECIPE

A great breakfast or quick snack is the Avocado Berry Smoothie. It's packed with nutrients and flavor, mixing the creamy texture of avocados with sweet berries that are filled with antioxidants. The omega-3 fatty acids, fiber, vitamins also make this drink anti-inflammatory so if you need something refreshing in your life then give it a try!

Servings: 2
Preparation: 5 minutes
Cook time: 0 minutes
Recipe Type: BEVERAGE

AVOCADO BERRY SMOOTHIE – BREAKFAST

Ingredients:

- 1 ripe avocado, peeled and pitted
- 1 cup mixed berries (such as strawberries, blueberries, raspberries, and blackberries), fresh or frozen
- 1 cup fresh spinach leaves (optional, for added nutrients)
- 1 cup almond milk (or any plant-based milk of your choice)
- 1 tablespoon honey or maple syrup (optional, for added sweetness)
- Ice cubes (optional, for a colder smoothie)

Instructions:

Combine Ingredients:

- In a blender, add the avocado, mixed berries, spinach (if using), almond milk, and honey or maple syrup.

Blend:

- Blend on high speed until smooth. If the mixture is too thick, add more almond milk to achieve your desired consistency. If using fresh berries and you prefer a colder smoothie, add a handful of ice cubes and blend again.

Serve:

- Pour the smoothie into glasses and serve immediately for the freshest taste.

Nutritional Information (per serving): Calories: 240 Protein: 3g, Fat: 15g (Saturated: 2g, Omega-3: approx. 0.2 g) Carbohydrates: 27g, Fiber: 7g, Sugar: 15g (natural sugars from fruits, additional if sweetener is added) Sodium: 70mg

Chef's Tips:

1. To improve the protein content, you can add a scoop of your preferred powder or a tablespoon of chia seeds to the blender before mixing.
2. For more anti-inflammatory properties, include a small piece of fresh ginger or a teaspoon of ground turmeric in the blend.
3. If you use frozen berries, it will make the smoothie thicker and more like ice cream – especially good on hot days.

ABOUT THIS RECIPE

Pumpkin Porridge is a hot, comforting breakfast that is filled with anti-inflammatory properties, which are provided by pumpkin, beta-carotene and fiber-rich veggie. It also has oatmeal that is good for the heart because of its ability to keep digestive system healthy and reduce inflammation at once. If you want to have more energy in the morning or need something nutritious during cold weather this dish will be perfect for you as it can give both taste and nutrition.

Servings: 2
Preparation: 5 minutes
Cook time: 10 minutes
Recipe Type: BREAKFAST

PUMPKIN OATMEAL – BREAKFAST

Ingredients:
- 1 cup rolled oats
- 1 cup pure pumpkin puree (not pumpkin pie filling)
- 2 cups almond milk (or any milk of your choice)
- 1/2 teaspoon cinnamon
- 1/4 teaspoon nutmeg
- 1 tablespoon maple syrup (or to taste)
- Optional toppings: chopped nuts (such as pecans or walnuts), a sprinkle of chia seeds, additional cinnamon, or a dollop of Greek yogurt

Instructions:

Combine Ingredients:
- In a medium saucepan, bring the almond milk to a boil. Add the oats and reduce the heat to a simmer.
- Stir in the pumpkin puree, cinnamon, and nutmeg. Cook for about 5-7 minutes, stirring occasionally, until the oats are soft and the mixture has thickened to your liking.

Sweeten:
- Once the oatmeal is cooked, remove from heat and stir in the maple syrup. Adjust the sweetness according to your preference.

Serve:
- Divide the oatmeal between two bowls.
- Add any additional toppings like chopped nuts, chia seeds, a sprinkle of cinnamon, or a dollop of Greek yogurt for extra protein.

Nutritional Information (per serving): Calories: 280, Protein: 6g, Fat: 5g (Saturated: 0.5g), Carbohydrates: 53g Fiber: 8g, Sugar: 12g (includes maple syrup), Sodium: 80mg

Chef's Tips:
1. To add more taste and health advantages, blend a spoon of ground flaxseed or hemp seeds with the oats.
2. If you would like it to be creamier in texture, use water and milk combined instead of just milk when preparing the oats.
3. Create a bigger portion at the start of each week then warm up servings as needed for fast and easy breakfasts all week long.

ABOUT THIS RECIPE

The Toasted Almond Butter and Banana Sandwich is a healthy, quick snack or breakfast option. It combines the smoothness of almond butter with the sweetness of banana between two slices of whole-grain bread. Packed with good fats, protein and fiber that fight inflammation while giving long-lasting energy.

Servings: 1
Preparation: 5 minutes
Cook time: 5 minutes
Recipe Type: SNACK

TOASTED ALMOND BUTTER AND BANANA SANDWICH – BREAKFAST

Ingredients:
- 2 slices of whole-grain bread
- 2 tablespoons almond butter
- 1 medium banana, sliced
- 1 teaspoon honey (optional)
- A sprinkle of cinnamon (optional)

Instructions:

Toast the Bread:
- Place the whole-grain bread slices in a toaster or on a skillet over medium heat. Toast until the bread is golden and crispy on each side.

Assemble the Sandwich:
- Spread the almond butter evenly over one slice of toasted bread.
- Arrange the sliced banana on top of the almond butter.
- Drizzle with honey and sprinkle with cinnamon if using.
- Top with the second slice of toasted bread.

Serve:
- Cut the sandwich in half or into quarters and serve immediately.

Nutritional Information (per serving): Calories: 410, Protein: 12g, Fat: 18g (Saturated: 2g), Carbohydrates: 53g, Fiber: 8g, Sugar: 20g, Sodium: 320mg

Chef's Tips:
1. To give it a more nutty taste and crispy texture, you can try to put some toasted almonds on the banana before sealing the sandwich.
2. For higher protein content, Greek yoghurt or chia seeds may be used as an alternative layer.
3. Another way to make things more exciting is by replacing almond butter with different types of nuts such as cashews or peanuts.

ABOUT THIS RECIPE

This Green Detox Smoothie is packed with nutrients, which are known to alleviate inflammatory responses and cleanse the system through their rich antioxidant properties. It's an ideal drink for a morning booster or a cooling post-workout snack; this smoothie incorporates different types of leafy greens and fruits that make it compatible with any anti-inflammatory meal plan.

Servings: 2
Preparation: 5 minutes
Cook time: 0 minutes
Recipe Type: Beverage / Smoothie

GREEN DETOX SMOOTHIE – BREAKFAST

Ingredients:

- 1 cup fresh spinach leaves
- ½ cucumber, chopped
- 1 green apple, cored and sliced
- ½ avocado, peeled and pitted
- Juice of 1 lemon
- 1 inch piece of ginger, peeled and minced
- 1 tablespoon chia seeds
- 1 cup coconut water or plain water
- Ice cubes (optional for a colder smoothie)

Instructions:

Prepare Ingredients:

- Wash the spinach, cucumber, and apple thoroughly. Chop the cucumber and slice the apple. Peel and pit the avocado. Peel and mince the ginger.

Blend the Smoothie:

- In a blender, combine the spinach, cucumber, apple, avocado, lemon juice, ginger, chia seeds, and coconut water. Add ice if desired. Blend on high until smooth and creamy.

Serve:

- Pour the smoothie into glasses and serve immediately for the freshest taste and most nutrients.

Nutritional Information (per serving): Calories: 180, Protein: 3g, Fat: 9g (Saturated: 1.5g), Carbohydrates: 25g Fiber: 7g, Sugar: 13g (natural sugars from fruits), Sodium: 60mg

Chef's Tips:

1. To keep yourself satisfied for a longer period of time, think about throwing in a spoonful of your most liked protein powder made from plants.
2. If you like your smoothies sweeter, you can add a little bit of honey or agave syrup, but the natural sweetness from the apple and coconut water is usually enough for most people.
3. This smoothie is meant to be consumed right away after blending so that the maximum amount of nutrients and enzymes are obtained from the fresh ingredients.

ABOUT THIS RECIPE

This light and nutritious recipe for an omelette with spinach and mushrooms contains many anti-inflammatory substances. Suitable for breakfast or lunch, this dish blends protein-filled egg whites with fibre-rich veggies such as spinach and antioxidant-laden food like mushrooms – perfect if you're trying to fight inflammation while staying healthy!

Servings: 1
Preparation: 5 minutes
Cook time: 10 minutes
Recipe Type: BREAKFAST

EGG WHITE OMELET WITH SPINACH AND MUSHROOMS – BREAKFAST

Ingredients:

- 3 egg whites
- 1 cup fresh spinach, washed and roughly chopped
- ½ cup mushrooms, thinly sliced
- 1 tbsp olive oil
- Salt and freshly ground black pepper, to taste
- Optional: herbs such as thyme or parsley for added flavor
- Optional: a sprinkle of turmeric for extra anti-inflammatory benefits

Instructions:

Prepare the Ingredients:

- Heat the olive oil in a non-stick skillet over medium heat.
- Add the sliced mushrooms and sauté until they begin to brown, about 3-4 minutes.
- Add the chopped spinach and cook until wilted, approximately 2 minutes.

Make the Omelet:

- Heat the olive oil in a non-stick skillet over medium heat.
- Add the sliced mushrooms and sauté until they begin to brown, about 3-4 minutes.
- Add the chopped spinach and cook until wilted, approximately 2 minutes.

Fold and Serve:

- Carefully fold the omelet in half using a spatula.
- Slide the omelet onto a plate and garnish with fresh herbs if desired.

Nutritional Information (per serving): Calories: 180, Protein: 14g, Fat: 12g (Saturated: 2g), Carbohydrates: 3g Fiber: 1g, Sodium: 200mg

Chef's Tips:

1. Carefully fold the omelet in half using a spatula.
2. Slide the omelet onto a plate and garnish with fresh herbs if desired.

ABOUT THIS RECIPE

This Apple and Cinnamon Oatmeal is a comforting dish that uses the natural sweetness of apples to create a spicy cinnamon flavor. It's perfect for any morning because it is not only yummy, but also has anti-inflammatory properties due to the antioxidants in oats rich in fiber and cinnamon. This meal supports good health all over while still filling up your hunger at daybreak, making it great for breakfasts designed around heart health!

Servings: 2
Preparation: 5 minutes
Cook time: 10 minutes
Recipe Type: BREAKFAST

OATMEAL WITH APPLES AND CINNAMON – BREAKFAST

Ingredients:
- 1 cup rolled oats
- 2 cups water or milk (dairy or plant-based)
- 1 large apple, peeled and diced
- 1 tsp ground cinnamon
- 1 tbsp honey or maple syrup (optional)
- ¼ cup chopped walnuts (optional)
- Pinch of salt

Instructions:

Cook the Oatmeal:
- In a medium saucepan, bring the water or milk to a boil. Add the oats and a pinch of salt, reduce heat to low, and simmer, stirring occasionally, until the oats are soft, about 5 minutes.

Add Flavors:
- Stir in the diced apple and cinnamon, and continue to cook for another 5 minutes, or until the apples are soft and the oatmeal is creamy. If the oatmeal is too thick, add a little more water or milk to achieve your desired consistency.

Sweeten and Serve:
- Remove from heat and stir in honey or maple syrup if using. Serve hot, topped with chopped walnuts for added texture and a boost of omega-3 fatty acids.

Nutritional Information (per serving): Calories: 290 (without walnuts and sweetener), Protein: 6g, Fat: 4.5g (1g saturated, if using water), Carbohydrates: 58g, Fiber: 8g, Sugar: 15g (natural sugars from apples, additional if sweetener is used) Sodium: 30mg

Chef's Tips:
1. Whilst cooking oatmeal, people tend to add protein powder or ground flaxseed for more taste and nutrients.
2. You can choose Fuji or Honeycrisp if you want a sweeter kind of apple that isn't loaded with sugar.
3. What makes this dish even tastier is that when the oatmeal is cooked together with apples they become soft and fully ripe thereby giving off their inherent sweetness.

LUNCH

ABOUT THIS RECIPE

This soup mixes the nourishing power of broccoli with the heart-friendly fats contained in almonds to produce a smooth, fulfilling meal. Broccoli is a cruciferous vegetable famous for its cancer-fighting elements and antioxidants; on the other hand, almonds contribute extra anti-inflammatory properties besides giving the soup a nice feel and richness which improves its taste too. For those desiring an appetizing dinner which promotes general well-being as well, then this particular dish would be perfect!

Servings: 4
Preparation: 10 minutes
Cook time: 20 minutes
Recipe Type: SOUP

BROCCOLI AND ALMOND SOUP – LUNCH

Ingredients:

- 2 tablespoons olive oil
- 1 onion, chopped
- 2 cloves garlic, minced
- 4 cups broccoli florets
- 4 cups vegetable broth
- ½ cup raw almonds, plus more for garnish
- Salt and pepper, to taste
- **Optional:** ¼ cup nutritional yeast or grated Parmesan cheese for creaminess and flavor

Instructions:

Sauté Aromatics:

- In a large pot, heat the olive oil over medium heat. Add the onion and garlic, and sauté until the onion becomes translucent, about 5 minutes.

Cook Broccoli:

- Add the broccoli florets to the pot and sauté for an additional 5 minutes, just until they start to soften but still retain their vibrant green color.

Simmer:

- Pour in the vegetable broth and bring the mixture to a boil. Reduce heat and let simmer for about 10 minutes, or until the broccoli is completely tender.

Blend the Soup:

- Add the raw almonds to the pot. Using an immersion blender, blend the soup until smooth and creamy. If you don't have an immersion blender, carefully transfer the soup in batches to a blender.

Season:

- Return the blended soup to the pot (if you used a standard blender), warm through, and season with salt and pepper to taste. If using, stir in nutritional yeast or Parmesan cheese for added flavor and richness.

Serve:

- Serve the soup hot, garnished with additional chopped almonds and a drizzle of olive oil if desired.

Nutritional Information (per serving): Calories: 220, Protein: 7g, Fat: 15g (Saturated: 2g). Carbohydrates: 17g Fiber: 6g, Sugar: 5g, Sodium: 300mg

Chef's Tips:
1. Toast the almonds before putting them into soup, this will increase their taste and make them nuttier.
2. If you would like a less thick consistency, add additional vegetable broth or water until desired thickness is achieved.
3. This soup can be stored easily and kept in the refrigerator for 5 days or the freezer for 3 months. Reheat over heat or in microwave when ready to serve.

ABOUT THIS RECIPE

This Roast Beef Wrap recipe is an easy to prepare and fast to cook dish that combines tender slices of roast beef with spicy horseradish and peppery arugula all wrapped up in a healthy whole grain tortilla. This meal is packed with nutrients that help fight inflammation like glucosinolates found in arugula as well as anti-inflammatory compounds contained in horseradish making it perfect for hearty lunches which do not compromise on taste or nutritional value.

Servings: 2
Preparation: 10 minutes
Cook time: 0 minutes
Recipe Type: LUNCH

ROAST BEEF WRAP WITH ARUGULA AND HORSERADISH – LUNCH

Ingredients:
- 2 whole grain wraps
- 6 oz thinly sliced roast beef
- 1 cup arugula
- 2 tbsp horseradish sauce
- Optional: sliced red onions, for added flavor and crunch
- Optional: a sprinkle of black pepper

Instructions:

Prepare the Ingredients:
- Lay out the whole grain wraps on a clean surface.
- Evenly spread the horseradish sauce over each wrap, leaving a small border around the edges to prevent spillage when rolled.

Assemble the Wrap:
- Arrange the roast beef slices evenly over the horseradish sauce.
- Top with a generous layer of arugula. If using, add sliced red onions and a sprinkle of black pepper for extra flavor.

Roll the Wrap:
- Carefully roll each wrap tightly, starting from one end to ensure the fillings are securely enclosed.
- Slice the wrap in half diagonally to serve.

Nutritional Information (per serving): Calories: 350, Protein: 25g, Fat: 15g (depending on the cut of roast beef) Carbohydrates: 25g, Fiber: 3g, Sodium: 500mg (varies based on the roast beef and horseradish sauce used)

Chef's Tips:
1. To make it gluten-free, you can use gluten-free wraps which are sold at many health food stores.
2. Before wrapping the rolls, put some olive oil or lemon juice on top of the arugula to give it a better taste.
3. In order to reduce spiciness but keep the sauce creamy, blend horseradish with Greek yoghurt or mayonnaise if you like a less hot flavor.

ABOUT THIS RECIPE

Lentil and vegetable stew is a filling dish that can be enjoyed all year round. This stew is full of nutrients and different kinds of vegetables which are packed with proteins, fibers as well as many other things that can fight inflammation like lentils do. Also, there's no limitation to what types of veggies one can use here making this recipe very versatile while still being nutritious and anti-inflammatory at the same time.

Servings: 4
Preparation: 15 minutes
Cook time: 45 minutes
Recipe Type: MAIN DISH

LENTIL AND VEGETABLE STEW – LUNCH

Ingredients:

- 1 cup dried green or brown lentils, rinsed
- 2 tablespoons olive oil
- 1 large onion, chopped
- 2 garlic cloves, minced
- 2 carrots, diced
- 2 celery stalks, diced
- 1 bell pepper, any color, chopped
- 1 small zucchini, diced
- 1 teaspoon dried thyme
- 1/2 teaspoon dried rosemary
- 4 cups vegetable broth
- 1 (14.5 ounce) can diced tomatoes, with their juice
- Salt and freshly ground black pepper, to taste
- Optional: chopped fresh parsley for garnish

Instructions:

Sauté Vegetables:

- Heat the olive oil in a large pot over medium heat. Add the onion and garlic, and sauté until the onions are translucent, about 5 minutes.
- Add the carrots, celery, bell pepper, and zucchini. Cook, stirring occasionally, until the vegetables begin to soften, about 10 minutes.

Add Lentils and Seasonings:

- Stir in the lentils, thyme, and rosemary. Cook for a couple of minutes to allow the lentils to absorb the flavors.

Simmer the Stew:

- Pour in the vegetable broth and diced tomatoes with their juice. Bring the mixture to a boil, then reduce the heat to low, cover, and simmer for about 30 minutes, or until the lentils are tender.

Season and Serve:

- Season the stew with salt and pepper to taste. Let it simmer uncovered for an additional 5-10 minutes to thicken slightly if desired.
- Serve hot, garnished with chopped fresh parsley if using.

Nutritional Information (per serving): Calories: 260, Protein: 14g, Fat: 7g (Saturated: 1g), Carbohydrates: 39g, Fiber: 15g, Sugar: 9g, Sodium: 300mg (varies based on the salt content of the broth and tomatoes

Chef's Tips:

1. If you want a more delicious taste, try to put some red wine into the soup when you are pouring broth in it. Then, wait for a while until the wine evaporates and add tomatoes.
2. This stew can be kept frozen for a long time without losing its quality. That's why while cooking it is better to make much of this dish and freeze each serving separately so that on hectic days one could quickly warm up the ready meal.
3. To enrich with vitamins and minerals, put some chopped kale or spinach 5 minutes before turning off fire – these products contain many useful substances necessary for our health.

ABOUT THIS RECIPE

Whole Grain Toast Sardine Salad is a dish that brings together sardines' omega-3 fatty acids and crispy fiber-rich whole grain toast, making it healthy for the heart as well as nutritious. Sardines are great for anti-inflammatory diets because they contain many necessary nutrients which promote heart health while combating inflammation throughout the body.

Servings: 2
Preparation: 10 minutes
Cook time: 0 minutes
Recipe Type: LUNCH

SARDINE SALAD ON WHOLE GRAIN TOAST – LUNCH

Ingredients:

- 1 can of sardines in olive oil, drained
- 2 slices of whole grain bread, toasted
- 1 tablespoon of lemon juice
- 1 teaspoon of Dijon mustard
- 1/4 red onion, finely chopped
- 2 tablespoons chopped fresh parsley
- Salt and pepper to taste
- **Optional:** sliced cucumber, tomato, or avocado for topping

Instructions:

Prepare the Sardine Salad:

- In a bowl, flake the sardines with a fork.
- Add the lemon juice, Dijon mustard, chopped red onion, and parsley. Mix gently to combine. Season with salt and pepper according to your taste.

Toast the Bread:

- Toast the whole grain bread slices to your preferred crispiness.

Assemble the Dish:

- Spread the sardine salad evenly over the toasted bread slices.
- If desired, add toppings like cucumber, tomato, or avocado slices for extra freshness and texture.

Nutritional Information (per serving): Calories: 280, Protein: 20g, Fat: 15g (depending on the type of sardines used) Carbohydrates: 18g, Fiber: 4g, Sugar: 3g, Sodium: 460 mg

Chef's Tips:

1. To make the dish lighter, one can put lettuce or mixed greens in with the sardines. This increases the size and fiber of the meal without significantly increasing calories.
2. One way to improve the taste is by adding a few capers or olives into your salad mix.
3. Another idea is to use sardines packed in water instead of oil for a lower fat content. However, if you are following an anti-inflammatory diet then it may be beneficial to include some healthy fats from sardines in olive oil.

ABOUT THIS RECIPE

This Salad Tomato and White Bean is a refreshing, healthy dish that pairs juicy tomatoes with creamy white beans in a tangy dressing. It contains many proteins, fibers and antioxidants so it can be served as a good accompaniment or even eaten alone as a light meal. The simple ingredients used have an anti-inflammatory effect; this is attributed to the monounsaturated fats provided by olive oil which help lower cholesterol levels while also containing dietary fibers found within beans necessary for regulating sugar levels thereby promoting general well-being.

Servings: 4
Preparation: 10 minutes
Cook time: 0 minutes
Recipe Type: SALAD

TOMATO AND WHITE BEAN SALAD – LUNCH

Ingredients:

- 2 cups cooked white beans (cannellini or navy beans)
- 2 large ripe tomatoes, diced
- 1 small red onion, finely chopped
- ¼ cup fresh basil leaves, chopped
- 2 tablespoons extra virgin olive oil
- 1 tablespoon red wine vinegar
- 1 clove garlic, minced
- Salt and pepper to taste
- **Optional:** Crumbled feta cheese or shaved Parmesan for topping

Instructions:

Prepare the Ingredients:

- If using canned white beans, rinse and drain them thoroughly to remove excess sodium.
- Dice the tomatoes into bite-sized pieces. Finely chop the red onion and chop the basil leaves.

Assemble the Salad:

- In a large mixing bowl, combine the white beans, diced tomatoes, and red onion.
- Add the chopped basil to the bowl.

Dress the Salad:

- In a small bowl, whisk together the olive oil, red wine vinegar, minced garlic, salt, and pepper.
- Pour the dressing over the salad ingredients and gently toss to coat evenly.

Serve:

- Taste and adjust seasoning as needed.
- Serve the salad immediately, or let it chill in the refrigerator for 30 minutes to allow the flavors to meld.

Optional: Top with crumbled feta cheese or shaved Parmesan before serving.

Nutritional Information (per serving): Calories: 210, Protein: 8g, Fat: 7g (Saturated: 1g), Carbohydrates: 30g, Fiber: 8g, Sugar: 4g, Sodium: 200mg (varies depending on the use of canned beans and added salt)

Chef's Tips:

1. 1. To make it tastier, mix some balsamic vinegar and red wine vinegar. You can prepare this salad beforehand and keep it in the fridge overnight. The taste will become richer while the salad is marinated. To diversify textures and increase nourishing value, add chopped arugula or spinach to a handful of ingredients before serving.

ABOUT THIS RECIPE

In a cold day, this Sweet Potato and Black Bean Chili is an excellent warm meal because it is hearty and healthy too. This chili contains sweet potatoes full of beta-carotene and black beans packed with fiber which makes it nutritious. Furthermore, its combination of spices alongside different types of vegetables can help boost immunity as well as improve general health. It's good for us when we eat such dishes!

Servings: 4
Preparation: 15 minutes
Cook time: 40 minutes
Recipe Type: LUNCH

SWEET POTATO AND BLACK BEAN CHILI – LUNCH

Ingredients:

- 2 large sweet potatoes, peeled and cubed
- 1 can (15 oz) black beans, rinsed and drained
- 1 large onion, chopped
- 2 cloves garlic, minced
- 1 red bell pepper, diced
- 1 can (14.5 oz) diced tomatoes
- 2 tablespoons chili powder
- 1 teaspoon cumin
- ½ teaspoon paprika
- 1 quart vegetable broth
- 2 tablespoons olive oil
- Salt and pepper to taste
- **Optional:** Fresh cilantro, avocado slices, and lime wedges for garnish

Instructions:

Sauté Vegetables:
- In a large pot, heat the olive oil over medium heat. Add the onion and garlic, and sauté until the onion becomes translucent, about 5 minutes.
- Add the red bell pepper and sweet potatoes, cook for another 5 minutes.

Add Spices and Liquids:
- Stir in the chili powder, cumin, and paprika until the vegetables are well-coated.
- Add the diced tomatoes and vegetable broth. Bring the mixture to a boil, then reduce the heat and simmer.

Cook the Chili:
- Let the chili simmer, uncovered, for about 30 minutes or until the sweet potatoes are tender and the chili has thickened.
- Add the black beans and cook for an additional 10 minutes. Adjust seasoning with salt and pepper.

Serve:
- Serve the chili hot, garnished with fresh cilantro, avocado slices, and a squeeze of lime if desired.

Nutritional Information (per serving): Calories: 295 Protein: 8g, Fat: 7g (Saturated: 1g), Carbohydrates: 52g, Fiber: 14g, Sugar: 11g, Sodium: 700mg (varies depending on the sodium content of the canned products)

Chef's Tips:

1. For a smokier flavor, try including smoked paprika or a chipotle pepper in adobo sauce.
2. As the chili is cooking, mash some sweet potatoes and beans with the back of a spoon to make it thicker.
3. You can freeze this chili so you might want to consider making twice as much and saving some for later when you need a quick meal.

ABOUT THIS RECIPE

With anti-inflammatory elements which amplify its taste as well as dietary value, the Grilled Chicken Caesar Salad is a delightful variation of the traditional meal. For a nutritious lunch or supper choice, this salad combines perfectly cooked chicken with crunchy romaine lettuce tossed in a lighter homemade dressing of Caesar type.

Servings: 2
Preparation: 15 minutes
Cook time: 10 minutes
Recipe Type: Main Dish / Salad

GRILLED CHICKEN CAESAR SALAD – LUNCH

Ingredients:

- 2 boneless, skinless chicken breasts
- 1 head of romaine lettuce, washed and chopped
- ¼ cup grated Parmesan cheese
- Whole grain croutons (optional)

For the dressing:

- ¼ cup Greek yogurt
- 1 small clove garlic, minced
- 2 anchovy fillets, minced (or anchovy paste)
- 2 tablespoons lemon juice
- 1 teaspoon Dijon mustard
- 1 teaspoon Worcestershire sauce
- 3 tablespoons olive oil
- Salt and pepper to taste

Instructions:

Grill the Chicken:

- Season the chicken breasts with salt and pepper. Preheat the grill to medium-high heat.
- Grill the chicken for about 5 minutes on each side or until fully cooked and internal temperature reaches 165°F (75°C). Let rest for a few minutes, then slice thinly.

Prepare the Dressing:

- In a small bowl, combine Greek yogurt, minced garlic, minced anchovies, lemon juice, Dijon mustard, and Worcestershire sauce. Whisk until well blended.
- Slowly drizzle in olive oil while whisking to emulsify the dressing. Season with salt and pepper.

Assemble the Salad:

- In a large bowl, toss the chopped romaine lettuce with the prepared dressing until evenly coated.
- Add the sliced grilled chicken on top, and sprinkle with grated Parmesan cheese. Add whole grain croutons if desired.

Nutritional Information (per serving): Calories: 350, Protein: 34g, Fat: 18g (Saturated: 4g), Carbohydrates: 9g Fiber: 3g, Sugar: 4g, Sodium: 450mg

Chef's Tips:

1. Instead of traditional croutons, which will give you carbohydrates and roughage, try using roasted chickpeas that have been cooked in order to increase their protein content.
2. If you would like your dressing to be more like a cream sauce instead of just vinegar and oil, add some extra Greek yogurt until it reaches the desired thickness.
3. Before grilling poultry, try marinating it with lemon juice, garlic cloves and olive oil for enhanced flavor as well as tenderizing.

DINNER

ABOUT THIS RECIPE

Olive tapenade tuna steaks are cooked in a Mediterranean way that is not only delicious but also good for the body. The omega-3 fatty acids found in this fish along with its antioxidant content from olives makes it an ideal dish for those following anti-inflammatory diets. This recipe has strong flavors and easy steps which can be done by anybody thus making them suitable for healthy meals especially those targeting hearts.

Servings: 2
Preparation: 10 minutes
Cook time: 10 minutes
Recipe Type: Main Course

GRILLED TUNA STEAKS WITH OLIVE TAPENADE – DINNER

Ingredients:
- 2 tuna steaks (about 6 oz each)
- 1 tablespoon olive oil
- Salt and pepper, to taste

For the Olive Tapenade:
- ½ cup pitted Kalamata olives
- 2 tablespoons capers, rinsed
- 1 clove garlic
- 2 tablespoons fresh parsley, chopped
- 1 tablespoon lemon juice
- 2 tablespoons extra virgin olive oil
- Fresh ground black pepper, to taste

Instructions:

Prepare the Tapenade:
- In a food processor, combine the Kalamata olives, capers, garlic, parsley, and lemon juice. Pulse until coarsely chopped.
- With the processor running, slowly drizzle in the olive oil until the mixture is well combined but still slightly chunky. Season with black pepper to taste. Set aside.

Grill the Tuna:
- Preheat the grill to high heat.
- Brush the tuna steaks lightly with olive oil and season with salt and pepper.
- Place the tuna on the hot grill and cook for about 3-5 minutes on each side, depending on thickness and desired doneness.

Serve:
- Serve the grilled tuna steaks topped with a generous spoonful of olive tapenade.

Nutritional Information (per serving): Calories: 390, Protein: 40g, Fat: 23g (Saturated: 3g, Omega-3: approx. 1g), Carbohydrates: 3g, Fiber: 1g, Sugar: 0g, Sodium: 720mg

Chef's Tips:
1. Make sure you do not cook the tuna for too long; it is good to eat a little raw inside.
2. To make it more Mediterranean, include grilled vegetables or fresh salad in your list of accompaniments.
3. Blend the ingredients longer if you prefer a consistent tapenade.

ABOUT THIS RECIPE

Grilled Olive Tapenade Tuna Steaks are a type of food inspired by the Mediterranean region which can excite the palate and provide many health benefits. With omega-3 fatty acids found in fish such as tuna, and antioxidants contained in olives this recipe is perfect for an anti-inflammatory eating plan. The strong taste combined with easy cooking instructions means it would be ideal for any nutritious dinner that promotes cardiovascular wellness.

Servings: 4
Preparation: 20 minutes
Cook time: 45 minutes
Recipe Type: SIDE DISH

STUFFED ACORN SQUASH WITH QUINOA AND CRANBERRIES – DINNER

Ingredients:
- 2 acorn squashes, halved and seeds removed
- 1 cup quinoa, cooked according to package instructions
- ½ cup dried cranberries
- ½ cup walnuts, chopped and toasted
- ¼ cup parsley, finely chopped
- 2 tablespoons olive oil
- 1 tablespoon maple syrup
- ½ teaspoon cinnamon
- Salt and pepper to taste

Instructions:

Prepare the Squash:
- Preheat the oven to 375°F (190°C).
- Brush the inside of each acorn squash half with olive oil and season with salt, pepper, and cinnamon. Drizzle with maple syrup.
- Place squash halves cut-side up on a baking sheet and roast for about 30-35 minutes, or until the flesh is tender and easily pierced with a fork.

Prepare the Stuffing:
- While the squash is roasting, prepare the quinoa if not already cooked.
- In a large bowl, mix the cooked quinoa, dried cranberries, toasted walnuts, and chopped parsley. Season with salt and pepper to taste.

Stuff the Squash:
- Once the squash halves are tender, remove them from the oven.
- Spoon the quinoa mixture into the cavities of the roasted squash halves, packing lightly until all the mixture is used.

Final Roasting:
- Return the stuffed squash halves to the oven and roast for an additional 10-15 minutes, or until everything is heated through.

Nutritional Information (per serving): Calories: 325, Protein: 6g, Fat: 15g (Saturated: 2g), Carbohydrates: 45g Fiber: 6g, Sugar: 12g, Sodium: 30mg

Chef's Tips:
1. Consider adding chickpeas or shredded chicken to the quinoa mixture for an extra protein kick.
2. If walnuts are not available or you just don't like them, try pecans or almonds instead.
3. Prepare the stuffing ahead of time and store it in the fridge. This will save you time when you're ready to assemble everything, which is great for holiday cooking or meal prepping.

ABOUT THIS RECIPE
A dinner that smells good and tastes better, Rosemary Lemon Chicken with Roasted Brussels Sprouts is also highly therapeutic. It incorporates the anti-inflammatory nature of rosemary and the detoxifying power of brussels sprouts making it an ideal meal for those who care about their health or are on a diet. In addition to this, it is easy enough to be made during weekdays but fancy enough for guests.

Servings: 4
Preparation: 15 minutes
Cook time: 30 minutes
Recipe Type: MAIN DISH

ROSEMARY LEMON CHICKEN WITH ROASTED BRUSSELS SPROUTS – DINNER

Ingredients:
- 4 boneless, skinless chicken breasts
- 1 lemon, zested and juiced
- 2 tablespoons fresh rosemary, chopped
- 3 tablespoons olive oil
- 2 cloves garlic, minced
- Salt and pepper, to taste
- 1 lb Brussels sprouts, trimmed and halved
- Additional rosemary sprigs for garnish (optional)

Instructions:

Marinate the Chicken:
- In a bowl, combine lemon zest, lemon juice, chopped rosemary, minced garlic, salt, pepper, and 2 tablespoons of olive oil.
- Place chicken breasts in the marinade and ensure they are well coated. Cover and refrigerate for at least 30 minutes, or overnight for deeper flavor.

Prepare Brussels Sprouts:
- Preheat your oven to 400°F (200°C).
- Toss the Brussels sprouts with the remaining 1 tablespoon of olive oil, salt, and pepper.

Cook Chicken:
- Heat a skillet over medium heat and add the marinated chicken. Reserve the marinade.
- Cook each side for about 6-7 minutes or until the chicken is golden and cooked through. Remove from the pan and keep warm.

Roast Brussels Sprouts:
- Spread the Brussels sprouts on a baking sheet in a single layer.
- Roast in the preheated oven for about 20-25 minutes, until they are crispy on the outside and tender on the inside.

Simmer Remaining Marinade:
- Pour the remaining marinade into the skillet used for the chicken, bring to a simmer, and cook until slightly thickened, about 3-4 minutes. This can be used as a sauce for the chicken.

Serve:
- Arrange the chicken and Brussels sprouts on plates.
- Drizzle the reduced marinade sauce over the chicken.
- Garnish with additional rosemary sprigs if desired.

Nutritional Information (per serving): Calories: 345, Protein: 27g, Fat: 20g (Saturated: 3g), Carbohydrates: 11g, Fiber: 4g, Sugar: 3g, Sodium: 220mg

Chef's Tips:
1. When the chicken is marinated for more time, you allow flavors to sink deeper into it.
2. Make sure that the Brussels sprouts aren't on top of each other while in the oven because this will make them roast better and become crispier.
3. Serve this dish with quinoa or a simple salad on the side for a full meal.

ABOUT THIS RECIPE

This Thai Coconut Curry with Tofu and Vegetables is a vibrant, delicious dish that brings together the rich flavors of Thai cuisine with the health benefits of anti-inflammatory ingredients. Featuring firm tofu and a colorful mix of vegetables, all simmered in a creamy coconut curry sauce, this meal is not only satisfying but also great for reducing inflammation and boosting overall health.

Servings: 4
Preparation: 15 minutes
Cook time: 20 minutes
Recipe Type: MAIN DISH

THAI COCONUT CURRY WITH TOFU AND VEGETABLES – DINNER

Ingredients:
- 1 block (14 oz) firm tofu, pressed and cubed
- 1 tablespoon coconut oil
- 1 onion, thinly sliced
- 2 cloves garlic, minced
- 1 bell pepper, sliced
- 1 zucchini, sliced
- 1 carrot, julienned
- 1 tablespoon fresh ginger, grated
- 2 tablespoons Thai red curry paste
- 1 can (14 oz) coconut milk
- 1 tablespoon soy sauce (or tamari for gluten-free option)
- 1 tablespoon maple syrup
- Juice of 1 lime
- ¼ cup fresh basil leaves, chopped
- Salt and pepper to taste

Instructions:

Prepare the Tofu:
- Heat coconut oil in a large skillet over medium heat. Add cubed tofu and fry until golden on all sides, about 5-7 minutes. Remove from skillet and set aside.

Sauté Vegetables:
- In the same skillet, add onion and garlic, and sauté until onion becomes translucent. Add bell pepper, zucchini, carrot, and ginger. Cook for about 5 minutes, or until vegetables are just tender.

Make the Curry:
- Stir in the red curry paste and cook for 1 minute to release its flavors. Pour in the coconut milk, soy sauce, and maple syrup. Bring to a simmer and let cook for 10 minutes, allowing the flavors to meld.

Combine and Finish:
- Return the tofu to the skillet. Simmer everything together for an additional 5 minutes. Turn off the heat and stir in the lime juice and fresh basil. Season with salt and pepper to taste.

Nutritional Information (per serving): Calories: 350, Protein: 12g, Fat: 25g (Saturated: 15g), Carbohydrates: 20g, Fiber: 3g, Sugar: 8g, Sodium: 400mg

Chef's Tips:
1. For the greatest taste, try using coconut milk with full fat because it provides a more luxurious and creamy consistency to your curry.
2. According to what is in season or what you like, you may change the vegetables. This curry is also good with sweet potatoes, snap peas and spinach.
3. You could put in a chopped chili or extra curry paste if you want your curry spicier. Depending on how you like it, adjust curry paste amounts and other flavorings.

ABOUT THIS RECIPE

Baked Salmon with Dill and Lemon Asparagus is a light, nutritious dish that combines the rich flavors of salmon with the crisp freshness of asparagus. The anti-inflammatory benefits of omega-3 fatty acids from the salmon and the antioxidants from the asparagus make this meal not only delicious but also incredibly beneficial for health. Perfect for a healthy dinner, this dish is simple to prepare yet elegant enough for special occasions.

Servings: 2
Preparation: 10 minutes
Cook time: 20 minutes
Recipe Type: MAIN COURSE

BAKED SALMON WITH DILL AND LEMON ASPARAGUS – DINNER

Ingredients:
- 2 salmon fillets (6 oz each)
- 1 bunch asparagus, ends trimmed
- 2 tablespoons olive oil
- 1 lemon, thinly sliced
- 2 teaspoons fresh dill, chopped
- Salt and pepper, to taste

Instructions:

Preheat Oven:
- Preheat your oven to 400°F (200°C).

Prepare the Asparagus:
- Place the asparagus on a baking sheet. Drizzle with 1 tablespoon of olive oil and season with salt and pepper. Toss to coat and spread out in a single layer.

Season the Salmon:
- In a small bowl, mix the remaining olive oil with chopped dill, salt, and pepper. Rub this mixture over both sides of the salmon fillets.

Assemble and Bake:
- Place the salmon fillets on top of the asparagus. Arrange lemon slices around and on top of the salmon.
- Bake in the preheated oven for about 15-20 minutes, or until the salmon is cooked through and flakes easily with a fork.

Nutritional Information (per serving): Calories: 345, Protein: 34g, Fat: 22g (Saturated: 3.5g, Omega-3: 1.8g), Carbohydrates: 5g, Fiber: 2g, Sugar: 2g, Sodium: 180mg

Chef's Tips:
1. For the best taste and texture, don't cook the asparagus too much – it should stay bright and a little crunchy.
2. Mashing some garlic or sprinkling crushed red pepper over the asparagus can also make it more delicious.
3. If you want a more filling dinner, serve with quinoa or have it alongside a light salad.

ABOUT THIS RECIPE

A tasty and aromatic dish, Herb Roasted Lamb with Root Vegetables combines the deep flavor of lamb with the sweet, earthy taste of root vegetables. This dish is made anti-inflammatory by using herbs and spices having such properties. It's not only filling but also helpful in reducing inflammation. When you want warmth at night during supper time, these meals are perfect because they provide that as well as being hearty enough for a complete meal.

Servings: 4
Preparation: 20 minutes
Cook time: 1 hours
Recipe Type: MAIN DISH

HERB ROASTED LAMB WITH ROOT VEGETABLES – DINNER

Ingredients:
- 2 lbs leg of lamb, boneless
- 2 carrots, peeled and chopped
- 2 parsnips, peeled and chopped
- 2 small beets, peeled and chopped
- 1 large sweet potato, peeled and chopped
- 1 onion, quartered
- 3 cloves garlic, minced
- 2 tbsp olive oil
- 2 tbsp fresh rosemary, chopped
- 2 tbsp fresh thyme, chopped
- Salt and pepper, to taste

Instructions:

Preheat Oven:
- Preheat your oven to 400°F (200°C).
- In a large roasting pan, toss the carrots, parsnips, beets, sweet potato, and onion with one tablespoon of olive oil, salt, and pepper.

Prepare the Lamb:
- Rub the lamb with the remaining olive oil, minced garlic, rosemary, thyme, salt, and pepper. Make sure to coat evenly.

Roast Lamb and Vegetables:
- Place the seasoned lamb on top of the vegetables in the roasting pan.
- Roast in the preheated oven for about 50-60 minutes, or until the lamb reaches the desired doneness (145°F for medium-rare). Halfway through, stir the vegetables to ensure even cooking.

Rest and Serve:
- Remove the lamb from the oven and let it rest for 10 minutes before slicing.
- Serve the sliced lamb over the bed of roasted root vegetables.

Nutritional Information (per serving): Calories: 550, Protein: 38g, Fat: 30g (Saturated: 10g), Carbohydrates: 35g, Fiber: 8g, Sugar: 12g, Sodium: 200mg

Chef's Tips:
1. To get a richer taste, put the lamb in a refrigerator with garlic, herbs and olive oil for one night.
2. You should slice root vegetables into equal parts so that they cook evenly.
3. Should you desire; sprinkle some balsamic vinegar onto the veggies prior to roasting them.

ABOUT THIS RECIPE

Pasta Primavera with Olive Oil and Vegetables is a dazzling, nutritious dish that puts the spotlight on fresh spring veggies against the backdrop of rich olive oil. It's made using multicolored veggies and whole grain pasta – perfect for those who want an appetizing anti-inflammatory dish that is also good for their heart.

Servings: 4
Preparation: 15 minutes
Cook time: 20 minutes
Recipe Type: MAIN DISH

PASTA PRIMAVERA WITH OLIVE OIL AND VEGETABLES – DINNER

Ingredients:
- 12 oz whole grain pasta (such as penne, spaghetti, or fettuccine)
- 2 tablespoons extra virgin olive oil
- 1 small zucchini, sliced into half-moons
- 1 red bell pepper, thinly sliced
- 1 cup asparagus, trimmed and cut into 1-inch pieces
- 1 cup cherry tomatoes, halved
- 1/2 cup frozen peas, thawed
- 2 cloves garlic, minced
- Salt and freshly ground black pepper, to taste
- 1/4 cup freshly grated Parmesan cheese (optional)
- Fresh basil leaves, for garnish

Instructions:

Cook the Pasta:
- Bring a large pot of salted water to a boil. Add the pasta and cook according to the package instructions until al dente. Drain and set aside, reserving 1 cup of the pasta water.

Sauté the Vegetables:
- While the pasta is cooking, heat the olive oil in a large skillet over medium heat. Add the garlic and sauté until fragrant, about 1 minute.
- Add the zucchini, bell pepper, and asparagus to the skillet. Cook, stirring occasionally, until the vegetables are just tender, about 8-10 minutes.
- Stir in the cherry tomatoes and peas, and cook for another 2 minutes until the tomatoes start to soften.

Combine Pasta and Vegetables:
- Add the cooked pasta to the skillet with the vegetables. Toss well to combine, adding a bit of reserved pasta water if needed to loosen the sauce.
- Season generously with salt and black pepper. Cook together for an additional 2 minutes to allow the flavors to meld.

Serve:
- Divide the pasta among plates and top with freshly grated Parmesan cheese and torn basil leaves.

Nutritional Information (per serving): Calories: 390, Protein: 14g, Fat: 12g (Saturated: 2g), Carbohydrates: 62g, Fiber: 10g, Sugar: 7g, Sodium: 150mg

Chef's Tips:
1. In order to increase the protein content, add grilled chicken or shrimp to the vegetables.
2. Any seasonal vegetables can be used for this dish; it is perfect for consuming leftover veggies from the refrigerator.
3. Squeeze some lemon juice or shake some red pepper flakes on it, and it will taste more tangy.

APPENDIX A

CONVERSION TABLES

Volume Equivalents (Liquid)		
US Standard	**US Standard (Ounces)**	**Metric (approximate)**
2 tablespoons	1 fl. oz.	30 mL
¼ cup	2 fl. oz.	60 mL
½ cup	4 fl. oz.	120 mL
1 cup	8 fl. oz.	240 mL
1½ cups	12 fl. oz.	355 mL
2 cups or 1 pint	16 fl. oz.	475 mL
4 cups or 1 quart	32 fl. oz.	1 L
1 gallon	128 fl. oz.	4 L

Oven Temperature	
Fahrenheit (F)	**Celsius (C) (approximate)**
250°F	120°C
300°F	150°C
325°F	165°C
350°F	180°C
375°F	190°C
400°F	200°C
425°F	220°C
450°F	230°C

Weight Equivalents	
US Standard	**Matric (approximate)**
½ ounce	15 g
1 ounce	30 g
2 ounces	60 g
4 ounces	115 g
8 ounces	225 g
12 ounces	340 g
16 ounces or 1 pound	455 g

Volume Equivalents (Dry)	
US Standard	**Metric (approximate)**
8 teaspoon	0.5 mL
¼ teaspoon	1 mL
½ teaspoon	2 mL
¾ teaspoon	4 mL
1 teaspoon	5 mL
1 tablespoon	15 mL
¼ cup	59 mL
1⁄3 cup	79 mL
½ cup	118 mL
2⁄3 cup	156 mL
¾ cup	177 mL
1 cup	235 mL
2 cups or 1 pint	475 mL
3 cups	700 mL
4 cups or 1 quart	1 L

REVIEW

Dear Reader,

I hope you found your journey through the pages of my latest book both enlightening and enjoyable. As the author, Jennifer Philip, I'm always eager to hear what my readers think, and your insights are incredibly valuable to me.

If you could take a few moments to leave a review, it would mean the world to me. Your honest feedback not only helps me improve my writing but also assists other readers in discovering books that might resonate with them. Whether it's a line you loved, or a meal, every bit of your feedback is appreciated.

Thank you for your support and for taking the time to share your thoughts. I'm looking forward to reading your reviews and continuing to create stories that spark your imagination and emotions.

Warmest regards,

Jennifer Philip

Made in United States
Troutdale, OR
06/24/2024